T0225890

Migrating to MariaDB

Toward an Open Source Database Solution

William Wood

Apress®

Migrating to MariaDB: Toward an Open Source Database Solution

William Wood
Pacific, MO, USA

ISBN-13 (pbk): 978-1-4842-3996-4   ISBN-13 (electronic): 978-1-4842-3997-1
https://doi.org/10.1007/978-1-4842-3997-1

Library of Congress Control Number: 2018963756

Copyright © 2019 by William Wood

This work is subject to copyright. All rights are reserved by the Publisher, whether the whole or part of the material is concerned, specifically the rights of translation, reprinting, reuse of illustrations, recitation, broadcasting, reproduction on microfilms or in any other physical way, and transmission or information storage and retrieval, electronic adaptation, computer software, or by similar or dissimilar methodology now known or hereafter developed.

Trademarked names, logos, and images may appear in this book. Rather than use a trademark symbol with every occurrence of a trademarked name, logo, or image we use the names, logos, and images only in an editorial fashion and to the benefit of the trademark owner, with no intention of infringement of the trademark.

The use in this publication of trade names, trademarks, service marks, and similar terms, even if they are not identified as such, is not to be taken as an expression of opinion as to whether or not they are subject to proprietary rights.

While the advice and information in this book are believed to be true and accurate at the date of publication, neither the authors nor the editors nor the publisher can accept any legal responsibility for any errors or omissions that may be made. The publisher makes no warranty, express or implied, with respect to the material contained herein.

Managing Director, Apress Media LLC: Welmoed Spahr
Acquisitions Editor: Jonathan Gennick
Development Editor: Laura Berendson
Coordinating Editor: Jill Balzano

Cover image designed by Freepik (www.freepik.com)

Distributed to the book trade worldwide by Springer Science+Business Media New York, 233 Spring Street, 6th Floor, New York, NY 10013. Phone 1-800-SPRINGER, fax (201) 348-4505, e-mail orders-ny@springer-sbm.com, or visit www.springeronline.com. Apress Media, LLC is a California LLC and the sole member (owner) is Springer Science + Business Media Finance Inc (SSBM Finance Inc). SSBM Finance Inc is a **Delaware** corporation.

For information on translations, please e-mail rights@apress.com, or visit www.apress.com/rights-permissions.

Apress titles may be purchased in bulk for academic, corporate, or promotional use. eBook versions and licenses are also available for most titles. For more information, reference our Print and eBook Bulk Sales web page at www.apress.com/bulk-sales.

Any source code or other supplementary material referenced by the author in this book is available to readers on GitHub via the book's product page, located at www.apress.com/9781484239964. For more detailed information, please visit www.apress.com/source-code.

Printed on acid-free paper

First and foremost, I would like to dedicate this book to my son, Cam Carter, in that over many months there were times daddy could not do things that a four-year-old really needs to do. Someday he will understand, but for now I have lots of things to catch up on.

Next would be to my wonderful wife and her patience when I had to skip out on some family function, or something or another, in an attempt to get words on paper.

Finally, my boss, Phil Mazza, for providing me the opportunity to take on some interesting tasks and responsibilities. The fine folks at MariaDB for their database solution and allowing me to speak at their 2018 conference, and to the team at Apress for their patience and taking a chance on someone who has never done anything like this before. This dedication would of course be remiss without mentioning that none of this would be possible without the drivers for change.

Table of Contents

About the Author

 **William Wood** is an IT professional who has worked across many disciplines in his 18-year career. He started his work experience as a student worker for his school's engineering department, which ran the school's website, doing LAMP Stack work for database-driven dynamic website development. He has been working specifically in the database field for the past 10 years, first on a team that supported development infrastructure and release engineering where he became the Oracle SME, and then entering the working database administrator field in 2010 as a DBA, primarily working with and supporting Oracle and Oracle RAC in high-volume, compute intensive, and high availability environments.

About the Technical Reviewer

Ben Stillman is Director of Subscriber Services at MariaDB Corporation. He has over ten years experience with MariaDB and MySQL, and prior to that had several years of experience with Oracle Database and SQL Server. Ben is well-versed in migration challenges and has a good understanding of the various database platforms on the market and what each brings to the table. Ben resides near Columbus, Ohio where he enjoys spending time with his family and riding motorcycles.

Introduction

Migrating to MariaDB covers a wide range of topics that can be applied to many facets of the information technology industry in that the same methods and practices can be used in any type of migration and development project. There are many approaches to tackling a monumental task, and presented here you will find the strategies and methodologies that I have adopted over many years in the technology sector. This work follows a fictional company, FWP, and the leader of their database team, Vernon, through a database migration from Oracle to the MariaDB Open Source database.

The fictional portions of the story are based on many years spent in the technology sector as well as the educational endeavors that preceded them. The name of the company, FWP, was chosen entirely in jest for a comical take on what many will recall from their educational experience with the work examples and problems that all seemed to relate to one kind of widget or another. I grew to detest the widget and all that it stood for, so using it so widely says a bit about my acerbic sense of humor and wit. The story itself spans experiences and observations as seen throughout my career, to add a bit of storyline to what is many times considered the dry topic of technical information. It also provide a vehicle for explaining the how and why of many things that have been accomplished in a varied career, highlighting the successful migration from the Oracle database to the MariaDB database.

The more technically oriented reader may gravitate to a few chapters, while the project planners and managers might glean more by reading it in its entirety. Whatever the reader's strategy, there are many gems that can be gleaned from each chapter no matter their discipline or background. The first chapters provide the storyline and background for a small fictitious company that has a new solution that needs a more cost-effective solution for its database backend, and how the head of their database department went about making this transition successfully. Vernon and FWP are fictional, as are their solutions; however, I have made the same database migration successfully using the same methodologies, roadmap, and solutions as discussed here. This backend migration was completed successfully on many levels and is still ongoing at the time of this writing, which is part of why getting this completed was a struggle with the timeline and final product.

Many of the methodologies on display throughout this book have been around for a very long time. One of my favorites that seems to display itself time and time again is that of the age-old mantra of "Keep It Simple, Stupid", referred to as KISS. It is very much applicable today as it was twenty years ago as I was exploring my educational pursuits. This is something that I have seen overlooked so many times with overworked, over-obfuscated, and increasingly complex solutions for problems that could be solved in a much simpler manner, making the solution easier to maintain, support, and deploy. There are also many methodologies covered here that have been around for a long time and are enjoying a rebranding or a reemergence in more recent times. Hopefully KISS comes full circle as well, as I am a big fan of the simple and effective solution.

There are many ways that one could make this same migration, so the more important aspect of this work is the path to follow, and not get hung up in the solution as applied here. What worked well here may not be as efficient for a much larger entity with a much larger data set size; however, the roadmap will still be the same and the solutions as provided will work when modified to suit the tasks requirements. Using Oracle's own tool set in the migration of the data carried some weight, as these tools were already available within the database software. This meant no additional cost for software to do this work, making the migration even more fiscally responsible for any entity undertaking a similar task, arbitrary of the database they may be migrating to with few modifications.

CHAPTER 1

Drivers for Change

There are many drivers for change in the world of technology and business. We are going to look at a couple of those in the following chapters from the viewpoint of a fictional company that has come out with a new product while at the same time going through a licensing audit. These two catalysts caused the company, Financial Widgets Plus (FWP), to evaluate their current database solution and possible alternative solutions because the cost, along with the overhead of use, of the proprietary solution could no longer be supported or fiscally responsible. They needed a replacement that would propel their new platform into the forefront while allowing them to generate more revenue to drive and support growth.

We will follow this fictional company, along with the fictional head of their database department, Vernon, as they go through the evaluation process to implementation. The hurdles as seen by FWP are identical to what any small software company would see when going through the evaluation and development of a migration plan for moving away from a high-cost, proprietary, closed database system like Oracle to an open solution, which in this case is MariaDB.

Driver: A New Product

The world of data and databases today is full of complex solutions and ever evolving buzzwords. However, nothing can be more confusing and daunting than the underlying costs, considerations, and licensing abstracts

© William Wood 2019
W. Wood, *Migrating to MariaDB*, https://doi.org/10.1007/978-1-4842-3997-1_1

when considering a Database Management System (DBMS) or migrating one's topology from one solution to another. This can easily become compounded into a daunting undertaking, depending upon one's type of business and the requirements that lie within. In the following chapters and throughout this book we will be looking at a lot of the decisions, requirements, and special considerations from the standpoint of a fictitious company (FWP) that falls within the financial sector of the business world. There are two main drivers behind FWP looking at an alternative database solution, a new product coming into fruition and trying to leverage its deployment in a cost-effective manner, so we will be diving into a majority of the aspects of these changes.

The new product that we will be talking about was the brainchild of a newly hired database administrator, Vernon, with FWP. This software company has been around for many years, offering a highly customizable product platform to large entities within the financial world. The company had done well for these many years offering this highly customized service to these large-scale lenders within the ever-evolving financial world. However, these larger entities were beginning to evolve as well and were starting to bring this exact type of service in-house, so the days were numbered for providing this highly customized financial widget platform that we will refer to as the Custom Financial Widget, or CFW moving forward. The CFW platform and methodologies were severely outdated. It was also starting to cut into profits because each one of the solutions was not sharing a common code base; no processes were done in the same manner twice; and it required dedicated resources for each implementation, requiring that someone had the background knowledge to keep it moving along. It did not take a rocket scientist to see that if FWP continued to operate in the same fashion, that its longevity was limited and at stake. Vernon was not a rocket scientist and he saw this, but he also saw the possibilities of effecting change to FWP, which he had come to work at with the attitude of it being the last job of his career prior to retirement.

Vernon knew that the task of moving away from the CFW product line was multilayered and would be no easy task. The company had a "customize" mindset that had to change, and was so ingrained that it was effectually an uphill battle to even get some ear time for this idea to get traction. When Vernon presented his idea to the first person, the response was "FWP doesn't want to grow, it does not want more customers, because there is too much money to be made doing what we do." This was definitely not a warm reception to be sure. It also had some undertones of management practices he had seen previously in his career many times before, so Vernon sat on this for the time being and contemplated, waiting for the right opportunity. As he waited for this opportunity, there started to be some rumblings about this new idea being shopped around at FWP for a turnkey Widget, something that could be quickly deployed, easy to support, etc. It's amazing how that works in the business world, and this could very well be a topic for another book; however, we will go back to Vernon's next step trying to get this idea to fruition.

A few months later, while having a family dinner out with the General Manager (GM) of FWP, Vernon seized the opportunity to explain the full ramifications and scope of his idea. This involved developing a standardized engine for a new product line called Standardized Financial Widgets, which we will refer to here as SFW, with an easily repeatable and common code base as the heart of the product. Then all the best parts of the current CFW could be rolled into plug and play modules if you will, having a multi-tiered approach. For example, if a customer wanted to be able to have electronic data warehousing reports, then that was a pluggable module, and with some of the more advanced modules the customer could move up to the next tiers. The other methodology for tiering would be through the number of transactions; if a customer did not plan to process enough Widgets to make it fiscally conceivable, then they would have to pay more for the base service. Or if they wanted system of record long-term storage of their Widgets, that could be done as well, but also with an upcharge for the storage requirements. Suddenly we were talking about a viable solution that could target both large customers and small, along with everything in between. The beauty of this solution, and what Vernon thought was the biggest selling point, was that not only would it generate revenue, but also lower the risk to FWP. That's because, being able to target smaller customers, they would be reducing the impact of losing a customer due to circumstances beyond their control, and this really obtained the effect that Vernon was looking for with the GM of FWP.

The new SFW product really started to get some momentum after this, and the GM requested that Vernon be the database administrator (DBA) assigned to this new venture. Interestingly, this did not pan out for Vernon as he had hoped. Even though the first couple of meetings seemed to go well and he contributed some really good ideas on how to proceed from the database side of things, he was then removed from the project after the third week by none other than the same boss who said "FWP does not want to grow." There are battles throughout life and careers and so Vernon decided to bide his time even though this was a major setback for him. It was okay because the idea for SFW continued to move forward, although slowly and not without its hurdles, and a somewhat abstract portion of the concept came into being with the first few customers. This proved the logic and marketability of the new product; however, limitations started to be seen, with the biggest one being the current DBMS solution that FWP had been using for over ten years. It was a solid foundation once Vernon went to work starting to improve and slim down the footprint into a more stable, fast, and lean deployment. In addition, Vernon began taking a very proactive approach to database principles that previous administrators had overlooked or just never considered. There was only one problem, scalability, both fiscal and physical resource, as the DBMS of choice from a historical perspective for FWP was Oracle Enterprise Edition with Real Application Clusters (RAC) and Advanced Security Option (ASO).

Driver: Oracle Costs and Business Practices

Like many organizations in the financial sector, such as banking institutions, credit card providers, and mortgage companies, FWP built their digital footprint around the tried and true architectural solutions of the time. For the most part these solutions oriented around a DBMS running on System V UNIX variants like Solaris, HPUX, and IBM's AIX. However, luckily FWP had already initiated conversions away from the old System V Unix variants and IA64 architecture, choosing to adopt RedHat Enterprise Linux in its stead along with moving away from the old Itanium-based servers to newer and faster machines based on the x64 architecture. The Oracle DBMS had become the solution of choice, especially with the combination of Real Application Clusters for hardware failover and the ASO (Advanced Security Option) for encryption of data at rest providing a secure and robust solution for any organization that deals with data protection requirements. During the proof of concept for these deployments, Vernon ran some pretty intensive stress tests against Oracle RAC on the newer architecture with the expected results of the combination performing superior to the previous and outdated architecture. However, this notwithstanding, the Oracle solution came at a very steep price that has grown significantly over the years, as has the complexity of licensing these solutions due to the advent of constantly evolving technologies such as virtualization, hardware partitioning, etc. that have and continue to evolve at an accelerated rate.

One cannot fault Larry Ellison for coming up with the licensing errata as instituted by the Oracle Corporation, as this was an absolutely brilliant idea. All one had to do was look at the basics of Moore's Law to see that as the architecture and solutions grew at seemingly exponential rates, thus would the coffers of Oracle. One of the aspects about the Oracle DBMS that helped solidify it as a revenue generating machine was the proprietary solutions that it offered to solve many complex problems with built in capabilities, optimization engines, and fault tolerance that other vendors did not have. The only standard Oracle was willing to adhere to was their own; while many other vendors worked on and solidified standardizations like SQL-99, Oracle did everything their way. The result is a fantastically stable high-performance DBMS solution that works so well that many of its customers and end users shudder to think of what the results would be in migrating to anything else. So they continue to pay the exorbitant yearly price tag associated with what used to be the only high-grade solution on the market with the requirements for high-volume transactional processing in a high availability always environment. The mere thought of having to migrate large volumes of database structure and data, especially considering all the built-in functionality that may have been used with application code side solutions that were driven by the back-end database, is daunting. It was a monumental task that Vernon and his team chose to undertake, due to but not limited to, the following major points:

- The high cost of the Oracle solution(s)
- Having to run a mission critical DBMS on outdated hardware, because if they upgraded to a more powerful architecture with more internal processors, the costs incurred would be significant
- The Oracle pricing model does not fit a small to mid-sized company.
  - Buy Oracle products in quantity, then the pricing is much cheaper
- Customers cannibalizing revenue-generating audit approaches being employed over the last few years
- The sales approaches that open one up to be cannibalized

To really get an idea of the scope and breadth regarding the primary drivers for change that Vernon and the team at FWP were dealing with, we have to take a pretty hard look at Oracle licensing and costs to see if they fit within the requirements of their new emerging product. This new product, Standardized Financial Widgets, required scalability, stability, security, failover capabilities, and cost effectiveness in order to be feasible. They knew that their current DBMS solution had everything thing they required from a stability, failover capabilities, and security standpoint. However, no matter how they crunched the numbers it did not come out as the viable solution that fit from a fiscally responsible and revenue generating standpoint as far as cost effectiveness, which was directly proportional to and impacted scalability. To explain this further, we are going to have to dig into Oracle pricing and licensing models and how they affect the bottom line for a small to mid-sized company. This is not to say that the solutions the team at FWP reviewed and vetted are not or were not perfectly suited to the larger entities as well, but more so the problem being that Oracle's does not fit the latter.

Oracle DBMS and DBMS-related products, as well as other Oracle owned products, essentially have two licensing methodologies, which consist of licensing by Named User Plus or by Processor type licensing. Oracle's revenue generating gold mine over the years has been directly relational to the already mentioned idea of licensing their product by the number of processors, which is great for them, but not so great for a smaller company to be able to absorb. This processor licensing requirement can also be very confusing because there are different prices for different processors, different processor architecture, and of course different processor manufacturers. One must be very careful with either licensing methodology, as there are some traps that a company can easily be led down that will come back to bite them when the License Management Service (LMS) team comes knocking to perform an audit. The team at FWP had the experience of finding this out the hard way, particularly with the Named User Plus licensing, so we will delve into that first.

Named User Plus is defined as an individual authorized by you, the licensee, to use the DBMS software, and this is regardless of the activity or duration of use. This sounds good for a small company, even a small company with software that uses the database as the back end for storing and manipulating it throughout processing in comparison with having to pay by processor; however, do not be fooled by this. This is where the term "multiplexor" comes into play, and what this means is that if you have a device, such as bar code readers, even if they are using the same "Named User" account, they are considered separate and disjoint users. What one can derive from this, especially someone in Vernon's shoes having taken over the database department in mid stride of an audit, is that this also relates to database-driven software applications. In FWP's case, they provided software as a service to their customers, who at no time had access to the database in any way, such as direct user accounts via a command prompt or a database GUI tool such as Toad. All application processing was done via the custom database-driven web application that processed financial information, but that application code, according to Oracle's legalese was in fact acting as a multiplexor. There is a huge problem here that lies entirely upon Oracle and how the Named User Plus licensing was sold to FWP. This was perpetrated upon them not only by an Oracle licensed reseller, but also by Oracle sales employees as well in the form that in order for them to save money they could license their development and test environments as Named User Plus while having their production environment licensed by processor.

This is where it gets interesting in that Vernon had started looking at licensing a two-node Oracle cluster in a remote data facility in order to provide proof of concept and scalability for the new Standard Financial Widgets product. This was right about the time the audit began and was quoted with the same Named User Plus licensing methodology for this new development and testing environment by the company's Oracle account representative. Under that guise, FWP, like most companies, generated no revenue from these types of environments, which was a significant break on the surface as compared with also having to license those non–revenue-generating machines by processor cores. The problem that soon came to light is that there appeared to be a lack of communication and interpretation between the Oracle sales and account representatives and Oracle's LMS group that performs the auditing.

According to the LMS team, FWP was out of compliance for their existing development and test environment. Because it too ran the same software as the production environment, these environments were also considered multiplexors and thus had an infinite number of users requiring years of back licensing fees for being improperly licensed. According to the interpretation of Financial Widget Plus's product, not just named accounts on the DBMS were considered, but so was every one of Financial Widget Plus's customer's employees as well as each one of their customer's customers. Not only this, but some licensing changes over the years also meant that Financial Widget Plus was also providing the Oracle DBMS software as a service to each one of these users, thereby meaning their licensing purchased needed to include a hosting license. What this could be interpreted to mean is that Oracle first sold a specific license in a way to make it seem like the customer was getting a break for their non–revenue-generating environments, but then several years later would schedule an audit with these same customers and charge them hundreds of thousands of dollars, if not in the millions, for improper licensing. This amounts to cannibalizing their own long-term customers to shake them down to increase revenue streams. Would a company really do that, and what could be done about it?

Vernon, as well as others on the management team, started to research this new problem and it appeared that this was exactly what Oracle was doing and people were starting to talk about it. Articles and tech websites were containing pretty in-depth pieces on this new strategy being implemented by Oracle while at the same time lamenting that there was nothing that could be done. If anyone tried to fight them in court over these sales practices, licensing changes, and interpretations, the behemoth of a corporation would tie them up in court for years. This could end up costing much more in legal fees and court actions only to possibly end up having to pay them anyhow. It seems that most of Oracle's customers came to this realization and would just cough up the money and purchase additional licensing per the LMS findings, considering it as a hard-learned lesson and moving on. Most came to the realization that the money to fight it wasn't worth it, and the costs and problems to migrate to another DBMS would be virtually impossible because they were so ingrained in the Oracle solution. Ultimately, this was the path that FWP chose upon attorney recommendations—to negotiate as the best outcome they could and keep moving forward, because it was against the odds to come out on top in this situation. However, the decision on how to move forward was a different story that would launch a change in FWP from the core.

This chapter would not be complete without getting into licensing costs involved at the processor level in regard to Oracle, as this is the real meat and potatoes of any company using an Oracle product in a similar fashion as FWP in a revenue-generating production environment where Named User Plus would be far and above the major cost. As already alluded to in regard to how Oracle arrives at costs via a multiplier value based on chip manufacturer, architecture, version, and type, please reference Table 1-1 as part of this overview. This is only a small sampling of the full table that Oracle publishes; however, it's enough to give one an idea of the complexity involved but at the same time not being overkill for the reader who is already all too familiar. The nuances at play here are not just related to a chip or its manufacturer, but also one that many will find interesting is the date purchased.

Table 1-1. *Sample of Oracle's Multiplier Information*

Manufacturer	Multiplier
Sun SPARC T3	0.25
SUN T6300, 1.4 GHz UltraSPARC T1 Processor	0.5
Intel Itanium Series 93XX or earlier Multicore chips(purchased prior to Dec 1ˢᵗ, 2010	0.5
Intel® Xeon® Platinum 81XX, Intel® Xeon® Gold 61XX, Intel® Xeon® Gold 51XX, Intel® Xeon® Silver 41XX, Intel® Xeon® Bronze 31XX, Intel Xeon Series 56XX, Series 65XX, Series 75XX, Series E7-28XX, E7-28XX v2, Series E7-48XX, E7-48XX v2, E7-48XX v3, E7-48XX v4, Series E7-88XX, E7-88XX v2, E7-88XX v3, E7-88XX v4, Series E5-24XX, E5-24XX v2, E5-24XX v3, Series E5-26XX, E5-26XX v2, E5-26XX v3, E5–26XX v4, Series E5-46XX, E5- 46XX v2, E5-46XX v3, E5-46XX v4, E3-15XX v5, Series E3-12XX, E3-12XX v2, E3-12XX v3, E3-12XX v4, E3–12XX v5, E5-14XX v3, E5-14XX v2, E5-16XX v4, E5-16XX v3, E5-16XX v2, and E5-16XX or earlier Multicore chips	0.5
Sun and Fujitsu SPARC64 VI, VII	0.75
HP PA-RISC	0.75
Intel Itanium Series 93XX (For servers purchased on or after Dec 1st, 2010)	1.0
IBM POWER7, IBM POWER7+	1.0

Using Vernon's two-node, single-cluster RAC environment at FWP as a model, he looked at scalability of this same architecture. The new product line was sure to take off and the one cluster running on the antiquated hardware would need expansion to a second cluster in the near future, so using Oracle's Pricing Guide this can easily be priced out. He planned on leveraging the same type of quad-core Intel processor to keep the costs down on the same model servers. From a security and compliance standpoint, this cluster would also need the same options as the existing one, so the following are the detailed requirements for this expansion cluster:

- 2 Dell servers

  - Single Intel Quad-Core 5640 at 2.67GHz

  - 124GB of RAM

- 2T of Network Storage

- Oracle Enterprise DBMS

- Oracle RAC

- Oracle ASO

- Oracle Tuning Pack

- Oracle Diagnostic Pack

- RHEL Licenses

This is Vernon's entire shopping list. However, we are only going to consider pricing from Oracle's published pricing list for the initial purchase of the required and necessary products based on the correct multiplier, from Table 1-1. For our pricing breakdown, refer to Table 1-2. Looking at the initial upfront cost using outdated hardware, it is pretty apparent that the upfront cost is fairly substantial: to be able to run databases on a single, two-node cluster comes out to $392,000. To be clear, this is only the costs for deployment; to be thorough in our analysis we also have to look at the ongoing costs, wherein with the way the chosen DBMS provider plays the game, they can and will change the rules of the game at any time. Table 1-3 provides a best-case scenario for yearly ongoing costs for upgrades and support at a cost of $86,240 a year. This is a huge amount of money that nearly makes scalability and cost effectiveness unattainable for virtually any small company hoping to use the Oracle DBMS solutions mentioned here and still be successful. It quickly became apparent, even with the audit tactics aside, that there had to be a better solution in order to provide a cost-effective solution to the customers of FWP, but cost was only a minor portion of the new mindset. In order to continue using the current DBMS and stay profitable, they were already having to run the software on no longer supported and outdated hardware at a risk of failure, along with no further updates and support. This also meant that any further deployments would of course need to be on that same hardware.

Table 1-2. *Pricing Analysis: New 2-Node Cluster*

Product	Multiplier	Units	Price per Unit	Total
Enterprise DBMS	.5	4	47,500	190,000
RAC	.5	4	23,000	92,000
ASO	.5	4	15,000	60,000
Diagnostic Pack	.5	4	7,500	30,000
Tuning Pack	.5	4	5,000	20,000
			Grand Total:	**$392,000**

The findings of Vernon's analysis and cost projections further presented the fact that the Oracle DBMS was just not targeted for the smaller companies like them, thus opening up an entirely new round of further research and analysis in regard to finding an alternative solution. There had to be a better way. This was a losing battle when coupled with the results of the audit findings and moving forward being forced also to pay the premium processor licensing for their development and test environments, which generated no revenue but were a necessity. How could FWP move forward, remain profitable, provide a cost-effective solution, and still survive? At the bottom line were a full analysis on what did they really need in a DBMS solution, could they possibly migrate to a completely different system, and at what cost. Certainly, there had to be risks involved. And after so many years of customized code and solutions, where no one thing was done the same way twice, how much time would be lost to working on a new back-end solution with code that for the most part had been developed specifically to **use** the Oracle DBMS? The magnitude of a change like this has been where a lot of the companies have balked: larger companies with much deeper pockets and multiple revenue streams. So how could a small company tackle what they could not? We will find out in the following chapters how they not only managed to make this transition, but took advantage of it and used it as a catalyst for change and came out the other side in a much better position with a much better product offering.

Table 1-3. *Pricing Analysis forOngoing Costs: New 2-Node Cluster*

Product	Multiplier	Units	Price per Unit	Total
Enterprise DBMS	.5	4	10,450	41,800
RAC	.5	4	5,060	20,240
ASO	.5	4	3,300	13,200
Diagnostic Pack	.5	4	1,650	6,600
Tuning Pack	.5	4	1,100	4,400
			Grand Total:	**$86,240**

The costs savings for FWP in migrating away from the closed Oracle proprietary solution is substantial and makes a very strong case for moving forward. Identifying risks and fulfilling requirements for their needs from a security and compliance standpoint would be the next step for the database team.

CHAPTER 2

Requirements and Risk Assessment

The primary catalysts for Financial Widgets Plus (FWP) to make such a monumental change were identified—the primary problem being centered on the ongoing and escalating costs over time of doing business with their current vendor. The benefits of their current DBMS being rock solid, dependable, and having served their needs effectively for many years, were revenue drivers going to be worth the risk to the company would be the next set of questions that would have to be answered.

The best approach for Vernon from a business standpoint was to mitigate risks through requirements. The financial sector has to deal with many auditing and security requirements; if the MariaDB solution could satisfy the same exacting auditing requirements as their current DBMS, then the data security risks would be mitigated by the requirements. Compromised data can bring about the end of a company in one fell swoop, and this was not a risk anyone was willing to take.

Once requirements can be satisfied, the next question is whether or not the level of effort (LOE) will be a risk to the continued operational needs and something that the company can withstand. FWP already had a large number of existing customers on the heavily customized platforms, along with an array of new customers on their standardized platform, that would have to be maintained and supported throughout

© William Wood 2019
W. Wood, *Migrating to MariaDB*, https://doi.org/10.1007/978-1-4842-3997-1_2

the same time period that it would take to implement the MariaDB
solution and integrate it into their code base. In culmination of the
project, these existing customers would then have to be migrated to the
new solution.

The project would undoubtedly need to be a success, otherwise
the time spent would be time lost for the small company and could be
detrimentally a waste of resources that could have been better used
elsewhere. This is why it was approached in a cautious and phased roll out
in order to be able to pull the plug at the first sign of a showstopper.

Requirements of a New DBMS

The team at FWP, through in-depth analysis and pricing models, quickly
came to the conclusion that their current database solution lacked the
scalability requirements by the limiting factor of cost. Sure, they could
continue to use their current solution—it worked well, was fast, and
provided high availability as a solid and sound solution—however, the
costs were phenomenal and would not allow them to target the business
they were going after. Historically their customers dictated and had
requirements that were specifically contracted around Oracle and Oracle
RAC for the security, high availability, and failover capabilities. They were
also willing to carry part of that cost; however, with the evolving and ever-
changing landscape of the financial industry this was starting to change.
This change was not just big customers changing the way they do business
and moving these financial services in-house, but smaller companies,
small lenders, service providers, and financial-oriented industries were
starting to look for solutions in order to complete loan origination and
credit decisioning for their own products and services.

The latter was a budding niche, and this was part of what FWP was targeting with their new standardized software. Something that was quick to deploy, standardized for ease of maintenance and support, modularly adaptable for more advanced capabilities and services, customizable for those willing to pay the price, but affordable for those smaller entities to leverage just as easily. This is what the organization of FWP was looking to capitalize on by reworking their legacy coding practices and processes to bring a solution to market that could reach virtually any sized potential customer. However, the costs of the Oracle line of products were in the way of this coming through to fruition in the longer term. FWP started to hear something from these new targeted customers that they had never heard before, which also ventured away from their current solution, and that was that they didn't care about what vendor's database solution they used. They just needed the service to be cost effective to them, quickly deployed, and capable of getting them up and operational and processing transactions quickly, consistently, and with as little down time as possible. This opened the doors to a much larger base of solutions to choose from for Vernon and the team at FWP, because no longer was the customer dictating that they must use expensive proprietary DBMS solutions like Oracle, SAP, Informix, and the like that previously had the market cornered for the financial sector.

This opened the flood gates for potential solutions, which Vernon was quickly finding out to have almost the same price points with every well-known proprietary DBMS solution provider. He had already vetted several of the big names as potential replacements for Oracle. Each big database vendor had a slightly different methodology in regard to their pricing models; however, once one went through this model one thing always came out to be almost identical. The price, even though a different pathway, computational model, or whatever one wishes to call it always worked out to be nearly identical. This meant that, sure, FWP could get away from Oracle, but they could not get away from the uncanny similarity in pricing. This all changed radically with the comments and viewpoints that they were getting back from these new customers and potential customers, that resoundingly they didn't care about the DBMS as long as their data wasn't stolen or used for nefarious purposes. The box was now open for a potentially drastic shift towards a cost effective Open Source solution and the time was right.

As we have already learned, FWP had already shifted away from the System V solutions for the server architecture and had replaced it with RedHat Enterprise Edition running on Intel x86 64-bit machines, so the next logical step was to target the possibility of an Open Source database solution as long as it fulfilled their requirements and those they set for their customers. Being in the financial sector brings about a myriad of rules and regulations that are always changing and ever evolving, kind of like technology, but had the technology from the Open Source community evolved enough to make one of the vendor-offered solutions a viable candidate was the question Vernon was saddled with answering.

Since the Standardized Financial Widgets (SFW) suite of tools dealt with loan origination and credit decisioning, this made it mandatory for yearly audits from a PCI DSS and SSAE 16 standpoint. So this is where Vernon chose to start with developing requirements, not just for an Open Source DBMS, but for any new database solution that FWP might consider.

Audits and Compliance

In the financial and banking industry there are a whole slew of regulatory acts, commissions, and compliancy standards, some that overlap and some that are not pertinent specifically to Vernon's database requirements or to FWP. However, we'll take a look at a couple that are intrinsic to the company, focusing primarily on those standards that fall within their best interest to follow in the act of providing the highest level of security standards to their customers in their day to day operations. It is no longer a rarity for one to read or hear in the news the latest security breach where cardholder data, government data, and other forms of secure information have been stolen for nefarious purposes. This can effectively ruin a company, especially a small to mid-sized company that does not have the resources to withstand such an impact.

Often referred to as an onion, data security has many layers and those layers place Vernon and his team of database administrators (DBAs) at the center, so security is of optimum importance for them as well as the rest of the company. Even though securing data places many layers above that of the database, one cannot rely on any other layer when it comes to layered security. This understandably puts a database team as the last line of defense in protecting data. Protecting data from exploitation is only the beginning of a database team's responsibility; it must also be protected from hardware failures, loss of integrity, and corruption. These latter items are just as important, and we will highlight those after we look at the two main audits that FWP undergoes, and maintains their compliance with, from an industry standard practice. This also reduces the compliancy needs of their customers by being able to present audit findings to them from an accredited compliancy auditor, thus in some cases negating those same customers having to send out their own audit teams. This saves both the company and their customers the economic impact of time and travel to come on site and perform the same audit and compliancy checks for their own regulatory needs.

The first one we will take a hard look at is SSAE 16, short for Statements of Standards for Attestation Engagements 16. This replaced SAS 70 (Statement on Auditing Standards 70) in June 2011 and replaced the

Service Auditor's Examination with the Service Organization Controls (SOC) report, referred to as SOC 1, 2, and 3. There are two report types contained within each SOC of the SSAE 16 standard: the Type 1 and Type 2:

- Type 1 has to do with controls broken down to the micro level into a specific day.

- Type 2 takes a much broader or macro look at controls over a much longer period of time, with a minimum of six months.

  - This is where having a change management system in place is very important. It should be easily searchable, with reporting features for tracking all changes that are within auditing scope over any period of time.

Breaking each SOC down, we have already seen that there are two different types of reports, so now we'll break down the three different types of SOC as well. There are three SOC types, of which one can have two different types of reports for each:

- SOC 1 is primarily related to internal access controls over financial reporting.

- SOC 2 is a detailed technical review and analysis of the controls of an organization related to day to day operations related to availability, integrity, confidentiality, and privacy.

- SOC 3 is a higher level analysis of SOC 2, containing a generalized statement of opinion and assurances of an entity's control system meeting SSAE 16 SOC 2 requirements for public release.

SSAE 16 primarily deals with physical location and data access control standards, of which the majority of are handled above the DBA level. However, Vernon and his team must remain fully aware of those standards and how they relate to their systems, and that a viable DBMS solution must support.

The second main audit and compliance standard for which FWP is responsible to maintain is the PCI DSS, which is the Payment Card Industry Data Security Standard. This one has a much broader impact on the selection of a potential DBMS and on the day to day operations of Vernon's team, a primary focus of which is the encryption of data, both at rest and in transit to and from the DBMS. This historically was a big hurdle for many DBMS vendors and one of the needs that originally led the team at FWP to choose the Oracle Enterprise DBMS with the ASO option as their solution. It was also a contractual requirement of some of their legacy Customized Financial Widget (CFW) customers and at the time was considered a financial industry database standard secure solution. There are many requirements of the PCI DSS that could carry the makings of a book all on their own, and one is encouraged to take a deeper dive to become intimate with the standardization as a whole. However, we are only interested in the requirements related to Vernon's search for an alternative DBMS.

The minimum requirements for a possible alternative solution came down to a few very crucial aspects of the PCI DSS that had to be available for any solution to be considered:

1. It must support the encryption of data at rest.

2. The database must support the encryption of data in transmission.

3. The ability to safely rotate cryptographic keys in use as required.

4. It must support multitoken authentication standards.

There is a wealth of information regarding PCI DSS specifications and requirements easily found online; however, a few things specifically to note from a database perspective were documented by Vernon's team. Most of it is very straightforward and to the point; however, one thing to note is that the PCI DSS documentation will actually reference standards as defined by the National Institute of Standards and Technology, commonly referred to as NIST. So, while researching and creating one's own documented standards multiple browser windows as well as multiple monitors will come in quite handy, having plenty of monitor real estate should also be a standard specification as well for anyone in the computer industry. If we were to take a look at the bare minimum standards that the aforementioned items 1 through 4 address from the PCI DSS, we have the basis as to why these requirements were essential when looking for an alternative database solution.

In order to attain a full understanding of encryption, we need to cover the different types and the nomenclature that is used to describe the two different options for encryption and their shelf life. Asymmetrical encryption uses two different keys for encryption and decryption processes, whereas symmetrical encryption uses the same key for both. The different types of encryption methods each have a different requirement for the lifespan of encryption keys, commonly referred to as a cryptoperiod. The NIST document SP800-57 Part 1 Revision 3 covers both the different forms of encryption as well as the cryptoperiods for data and what we are specifically looking at from a DBMS table and tablespace encryption standpoint, which is Symmetric Data Encryption Keys and that they must be rotated with a maximum cryptoperiod of two years contingent on risk factors.

The ability to encrypt data in transit has been supported for quite some time with many Open Source database solutions by leveraging Secure Socket Layer (SSL) for creating an encrypted network link between systems. The encryption methodology used for SSL throws a completely different spin in that it uses both symmetric and asymmetric encryption keys.

Asymmetric Keys are used to initiate the handshake between the client and server; once the Asymmetric Key is validated the Symmetrical keys take over for the actual encryption of the data in transmission and decryption at the end point for entrance into the database. The acceptable cryptoperiod for both of these key types is also limited to the maximum lifespan of two years, also contingent on risk factors.

The dive into encryption requirements would not be complete without an explanation regarding mitigating risk factors related to a key's cryptoperiod. The same NIST documentation breaks this down into several external factors that require key rotations, as well as factors related to the key generation itself and the processes involved in their maintenance and deployment. A shorter cryptoperiod, one could extrapolate, would have the benefit of enhancing their security endeavors. However, this can become difficult to manage as well as open up the potential for other problems such as human error or disruption of service, therefore negating the benefits of the process and introducing additional risk. A DBA's worst nightmare would be to lock themselves out of their own data, which would be irreversible. As long as one's strategy uses strong cryptographic keys, fewer managed key rotations are actually much better and lower the risk much more significantly. That having been said, there are several factors that can warrant key changes out of the necessity for maintaining the security of one's data, with a couple of the most obvious being:

- Employee turnover, specifically for anyone with access to, or who was a part of, the encryption key process whether their departure was voluntary or involuntary

- An existing immediate threat to related systems; an example could be a hacked application server where access to the client keys have been exploited

The ability to rotate keys safely, therefore, is of great importance for both the encryption of data at rest and data in transmission. Developing a process to do this in a controlled and tightly managed manner is crucial, and any DBMS solution under consideration must have a stable and solid set of utilities in order to reduce the risk to the data throughout the process. Oracle has a very wide leveraged and vetted solution for this in their ASO product; however, even one of the oldest DBMS providers with such a secure system recommends changing encryption keys as infrequently as possible. This also confirms what NIST alludes to within its own standards documentation. One cannot make any more important recommendation than to have a well-planned and documented process for rotating encryption keys, specifically for data at rest, and above all having part of that process begin with a full backup of any database as the first step in the process.

Getting back to the team at FWP and their search for a cost-effective scalable alternative to their Oracle driven platform, Vernon's search when looking at proprietary big-name solutions was able to match every single one of these requirements; however, it failed the fiscal economic viability portion, so he turned his attention to the Open Source market place. While evaluating almost every solution he found that, although cost effective, they lacked a data encryption solution that made the migration a viable one. Many of them, such as MySQL, supported the novelty of encrypting columns. However, that had to be done at the application code level when creating the record for inserting by encrypting it, and then again at the same application level when selecting and decrypting the data out of the database. This was a nightmare, not just due to the amount of changes to make this work, but also for the maintainability of the encryption process to encrypt and decrypt the data with a possibly performance impact on the large data objects, which are very prevalent in both the CFW and the SFW platform.

In the middle of Vernon's search an interesting thing happened at the most opportune time: an Open Source database solution that was forked off of MySQL announced that their latest version would contain a solution for encrypting data at rest, not only at the column level but also at the full table and tablespace levels. The name of this solution was MariaDB, and the timing could not have been more perfect. With the announcement of MariaDB version 10.1 in the latter part of 2015, FWP finally had a possible contender.

As Vernon set about researching and evaluating the MariaDB solution, the possibilities really came to light with the potential that existed with a migration of this magnitude. With it being a fork of the MySQL database, that meant anything one could do in MySQL could also be done with MariaDB with such tools as Perl and the unlimited number of Perl modules, specifically the Perl DBI, and this was extremely exciting. In Vernon's early career he had done some database driven web development using Linux Apache MySQL and predominantly Perl, so he began to envision reworking legacy solutions and the implementation of standardized solutions, and the potential was limitless. To be able to have the opportunity to fix all the bad database side solutions that had propagated over the years with FWP would be a lot of hard work, but it would be time well spent. As long as the requirements could be met, the solution from MariaDB could be just what was needed to really effect change within the organization across the board.

At the culmination of a couple weeks of deep diving into the documentation for MariaDB, and cross referencing the wealth of documentation that had been around for years with MySQL, it appeared they had found their solution. MariaDB had the required encryption capabilities along with several other valuable options built in:

- Data encryption at rest was supported for three of the commonly used storage engines:

  - InnoDB

  - XtraDB

  - Aria

- Encryption of temporary files and binary logs

- Encryption key management:
  - Supported the use of multiple keys
  - Each key has a 32-bit integer as an identifier and can be versioned.
    - This allows one to change encryption keys automatically to newer versions.
  - Supports two encryption algorithms:
    - AES_CBS
    - AES_CTR

Things started moving very quickly now, as MariaDB also supported SSL for the encryption of data in transmission with the openSSL plugins and also supported multitoken authentication via RSA's PAM Authentication Agent. It appeared that there were no deal breakers that could be found from a PCI DSS requirements standpoint; however, we have to also look at the costs and if it will scale to handle the same kind of load as what FWP was currently running on Oracle. There were a lot of questions that still had to be answered regarding whether they could service the same number of customer databases with a similar database footprint or would they need more database servers, and what the cost ratio involved might be if it took more servers to process the same volume of information as one Oracle Cluster, so Vernon's last requirement was to compare the costs.

Looking at the comparison on a by server license scope was the next logical step. This was done by projecting the costs of a two-node Oracle Cluster running on their existing outdated quad-core systems vs. a three-node MariaDB Cluster using their Maxscale database proxy on whatever system and processor Vernon's team wanted to run it on. They did a five-year projection starting with initial upfront costs that looked at it strictly from a software licensing and support viewpoint based on similar solutions, and as we can see from Table 2-1 there really wasn't a comparison. On a per server case, they were looking at a very significant savings that would put them on target for the new SFW product's cost effectiveness. Even if the database collapse ratio meant more servers, the initial costs were looking very promising; however, further projections were needed for the bigger picture.

Table 2-1. *Initial Upfront Costs*

Product	MariaDB per Server	Oracle per Core
Enterprise Database/Proxy	7,500	47,500
Clustering	Included	23,000
Compression	Included	11,500
Partitioning	Included	11,500
Security/Encryption	Included	15,000
Diagnostic Pack	N/A	7,500
Tuning Pack	N/A	5,000
Firewall	Included	6,000
Data Masking	Included	11,500
Totals:	**$7,500**	**$138,500**

Looking at the difference in licensing scope really made this analysis stand out, because Oracle licensing is bound by processor cores and MariaDB is by server. This meant that not only could they possibly be on track to a much more cost-effective DBMS solution, they could run it on any type of server with all the CPU power they could find. This is huge, especially when one considers the potential for database collapse ratio going from one system to the other, which could be very minimal already; however, being able to run the MariaDB solution on high-end server

27

architectures had the potential to relegate that to being a fleeting thought. Vernon had already made the observation that with MariaDB with Galera clustering that the minimum number of servers in a cluster was three; as well, it would take another set of server licenses for the Maxscale product out in front of the clustered solution for connection routing and failover, and the price was the same for either product meaning at least five licenses. FWP was looking at an initial cost for a similarly licensed three-node Oracle Cluster coming in at approximately $831,000 running on antiquated quad-core servers, while the initial first year cost for a MariaDB Cluster, requiring three nodes for the cluster and two for the Maxscale proxy, came in at $37,500. The team was ecstatic!

The next step was to complete a full five-year project, even though the team already had a very good idea who the hands-down winner was going to be. Looking at Table 2-2 we can see that the costs over time are holding true to intuition in that one core for the Oracle solution is almost the price of the first-year cost of MariaDB. The full scope of the cost comparison between the two DBMS solutions for five years can now be computed with the information we have from Table 2-2. The results are phenomenal, and FWP appeared to have options for the first time in a very long time that could have a very beneficially positive impact on their business. As Vernon and his team sat back and reflected on the results of the cost analysis and double-checked their work, the flood gates opened in regard to next steps: where did they go from here, and how they were going to get there with as little risk as possible? One thing that can easily be construed from the following five-year cost analysis was that the offset in costs alone could very well pay for the change:

- Oracle 5-Year Cost: **$1,562,280**

- MariaDB 5-Year Cost: **$187,500**

Table 2-2.   *Yearly Licensing and Support Ongoing*

Product	MariaDB per Server	Oracle per Core
Enterprise Database/Proxy	7,500	10,450
Clustering	Included	5,060
Compression	Included	2,530
Partitioning	Included	2,530
Security/Encryption	Included	3,300
Diagnostic Pack	N/A	1,650
Tuning Pack	N/A	1,100
Firewall	Included	1,320
Data Masking	Included	2,530
Totals:	**$7,500**	**$30,470**

Risks

FWP had been around for over 30 years and over this time had been a very conservatively run business, and for them to take on the work involved for a change this huge had to come with some risk. So now that the team had come to the conclusion that they had found their new DBMS it was time to calculate the risks. It was apparent that MariaDB fulfilled the requirements as set forth by Vernon's team and was much more cost effective than Oracle. It was also scalable, not just from an architectural viewpoint, but from a cost to scale viewpoint as well. If successful, this new database backend could make the new standardized solution a real revenue-generating possibility at a time that couldn't have been better for everyone; however, any risks had to be evaluated and marginalized as much as possible.

Even considering migrating from a solution like Oracle's, high price tag aside, is something that many institutions would give a wide pass on. Not only was Vernon's team considering this, but the potential replacement DBMS was an Open Source solution, an Open Source Database Management Solution (OSDBMS) to be exact. The Open Source community has produced some really great tools and solutions over the years; however, many times they were lacking in areas that the proprietary solutions excelled at, worked flawlessly, and were much more polished.

A couple areas of concern that made choosing an OSDBMS for a financial sector solution a potential risk were documentation and flaky behavior, what many in the industry call undocumented features. Historically, Open Source solutions are not all known to have the best documentation; however, since MariaDB was branched from MySQL, which has been around for many years, where the MariaDB documentation might fall short there was a wealth of it available for MySQL. Even though Vernon found the MariaDB documentation to be pretty good and thorough, it also occasionally referenced MySQL documentation. This was a plus and relieved apprehension where documentation was concerned; however, the team was still at the behest of a fairly new technology stack that made up the solution. Encryption was first added with version 10.1, released in 2015. What kind of issues could they come across and more importantly how responsive would their support organization be with any of the aforementioned undocumented features? Needless to say, many of these concerns were set aside with firm assurances that they had a top-notch support organization that would be ready to offer any assistance that might be needed to work through any issues.

· The FWP team knew that many of the processes and capabilities that they took for granted with the Oracle's DBMS would not be available with MariaDB. Part of their analysis included that this would mean a more active role on the part of their DBAs as well as the need for additional staff resources to handle the extra work load that would be involved.

Vernon knew from past experience that they always ran very lean from a DBA perspective. He had actually spent a few years of working very long hours, nights and weekends, and being on call the entire time, with working 70 plus hour weeks not being unheard of. He had a young son and had spent the first couple years of his son's life working, so part of the consideration would have to be that the database team would need to grow. However, the days of the high-paid Oracle DBA were numbered, and his management was in agreement that staffing needs were understandable and expected.

To help offset many of the technical risks involved in a migration of this magnitude, they could also engage in onsite training and remote database services that were offered by MariaDB in part of their negotiations with them. The great thing about MariaDB training is that not only do they offer DBA training, but also for the development teams as well. These options were crucial and turned out to be of great benefit to both of these main groups relating to the new technology stack. With the cost analysis, being able to leverage the expertise at MariaDB as needed, training, and remote services removing the blunt of the risk the only other factor was time and resources being tied up, or in this case freed up to be able to work on the code side of the technology stack, the migration of the database design from the Oracle to MariaDB, and just as importantly obtaining the customer base for the new standardized product suit of offerings.

FWP already had several new customers running on differing amalgamations of their standardized product; however, they were running on Oracle. The fact that they already had customers on the solution meant the market was there. There were even more customers lined up that had the potential to go straight to the new technology stack, completely bypassing Oracle and never having to be migrated. This allowed the resources on the code and database side of the product to be allocated to make this work, and this would be no easy feat because the teams were already stretched very thin and all the current customers still needed to be maintained, supported, and new requests addressed. However, none of these considerations were showstoppers and the decision was made to move forward to the next phase of the project and taking a hard look at the scope of the changes required.

CHAPTER 3

Database and Application Code

With no showstoppers found with MariaDB, the next phase of validating the solution entailed taking a look at moving on to the implementation phase by evaluating both database and application code for migration to arrive at a feasible plan. Once the work was completed in the previous phase they were pretty optimistic and excited about the MariaDB solution; however, they wanted to analyze the process of not only adding new customers but migrating existing customers on the Oracle DBMS to MariaDB. The LOE was also a concern from the applications side as well as mapping data types, database code changes, and rewrites for PL SQL, and of course sequences.

From a database perspective the database team was not too concerned about anything from their side. There would be syntax differences, and Vernon knew they would have to code around packages and such that Oracle had built in but MariaDB did not. The sequences were not even going to be a huge hurdle, as they could be implemented to work similarly to Oracle with some PL SQL programming on the database side. The bigger question was the application code, and it turned out to be easier than anyone thought.

© William Wood 2019
W. Wood, *Migrating to MariaDB*, https://doi.org/10.1007/978-1-4842-3997-1_3

Migrating the Database

The team at Financial Widgets Plus (FWP) found that MariaDB contained the requirements they were looking for and so much more, all in one package, but there were still many unanswered questions. The biggest question had been answered, and yes MariaDB was viable and they had made it their choice; however, how they were going to get there opened up a copious amount of additional questions. It seemed easy for new customers to just start out on the new database once the code database and application side were modified to work. On the database side there were triggers, stored procedures, and datatypes to migrate, but Vernon and his team needed to do a deep dive into everything to get an idea of the scope of work involved. Certainly, there would be application code changes to interface and perform transactions with the new OSDBMS. All functionality would have to be available, or a new process would have to be created to perform the same actions just as they were currently being completed. It was now time to take a look at the scope involved and get a strategic plan in place to make it happen, while at the same time mitigating risk.

Vernon had an idea of exactly how to plan his approach to completing a task as monumental as this. In higher level mathematics and physics, one of the biggest and often overlooked side effects was learning to break what seemed like daunting tasks into smaller, easier to manage and solve tasks, approaching each one individually. Previous experience gave him some insight from having completed his share of successful Oracle migrations over the years, so Vernon was certain it could be done. Obviously this was going to be quite different, as he wasn't managing the migration of one version of Oracle to another, but migrating to a totally different database solution. It was a challenge he was eager to get involved in, so he started breaking it down:

1. Deploy the simplest architectural solution for proof of concept

2. Set up and test the technology that addressed the requirements

3. Assess scope of changes at the DDL and database side programming levels

4. Assess application side changes

As the analysis showed, their current solution came with an exorbitant price tag. This price wasn't just for the DBMS, but also individual prices for every piece of the solution required to maintain compliance and secure their customer's data. It was definitely apparent that if this project could be pulled off successfully, it would be a game changer for FWP, it's future, and its employees' futures. The outlook was one that suited the culture perfectly in that the money they could save by switching to a much more cost-effective system that fulfilled all the security requirements meant that they could get their pricing for the new Standardized Financial Widgets platform in line with the types of business they were targeting. This also meant the ability to have more economic resources to spend on marketing campaigns, staffing, and employee retention—all to ultimately go after more business, which would mean growth and a higher potential for leveraging the scalability of the new solution. FWP became a fully licensed customer of MariaDB in December of 2015, and there was a lot of work to do for Vernon and his team of DBAs. Not only did they need prepare for new business coming in on the new database, but the existing SFW customers would also have to be migrated data and all.

Vernon knew that they would need to get a MariaDB footprint within their datacenters as soon as possible, so the first item of order was to leverage the knowledge and staff of the MariaDB team. They were able to get one of the MariaDB consultants on site to help them make this a quick endeavor to get the new solution up and running as expediently as possible. This would save the team considerable time and provide the database team with an active deployment to get accustomed to and to start testing against with code that would be need to be migrated. This strategy worked out great and since Vernon was able to work one on one with the consultant, it turned out to not only be valuable for getting their first set of servers up and running with the new OSDBMS, but a wealth of knowledge was shared in the process. This turned out to be well worth the effort, and the professional staff at MariaDB were just as excited about their solution as the team at FWP was. They are legitimately there to help their customers to succeed.

It only took a few days until they had a fully functional set of MariaDB servers set up, and not just replicating locally but also replicating successfully to their remote data center on the other side of the country. This was some major progress considering the time that elapsed from the initial evaluation to having it live and in the FWP data centers, and this gave the entire team an extremely optimistic outlook. They had successfully set up four database servers, three at their local data center and one in the remote location, and two Maxscale servers with very few problems. The setup leveraged the following resources that fulfilled their audit compliance:

- Data encryption at rest

- Data encryption in transmission with SSL

- Multitoken authentication using the RSA PAM plugin

It wasn't completely trouble free, but the few things they ran into were minimal and each time they found a way to work around any problems. The next phase was to test the features with encryption and the ability to change and rotate encryption keys as their requirements dictated, which went smoothly without any problems. One of the issues they did run into was regarding the use of PAM for RSA authentication. It required local user accounts to initiate the authentication process with, and from a historical standpoint the only users that had accounts local to any database servers were limited strictly to those users that were necessary and business needs dictated. This meant the following teams:

- Systems team

- Networking team

- Security team
- Database team

The way that Vernon was able to resolve the issue with PAM authentication was to work with the systems and security teams for the creation of the accounts, but with no local login capabilities. Having previous systems administration experience prior to becoming a full-fledged database administrator (DBA), he knew that they could create accounts local to the servers in Linux; however, they could also prohibit those accounts from being able to log in locally, but this would still allow them to authenticate. Once the accounts were created and set up to prohibit local login, they tested the setup and it worked flawlessly while not compromising security. Another hurdle they ran across also related to PAM and RSA was that the Maxscale database proxy did not support this type of authentication, which meant all internal users that required database access would need to connect directly to a database server and bypass the proxy completely.

The team had their proof of concept deployment and had tested the security requirements with great success with no showstoppers.

Database Side Programming

Following Vernon's task list meant that his next stop was a database side deep dive; however, since he had already been supporting legacy customers as well as new customers he was very intimate with the overall design for both. Much of both the legacy and new standardized solution did not rely on heavy amounts of database side programming. However, there were triggers, stored procedures, and various scripts that would need at least some reworking, with development, debugging, and testing time involved. MariaDB advertised a very high percentage of support for the PL/SQL language and most of the database side code was fairly straightforward and easy to follow, so there were not many concerns here. There were also some Oracle built-in functionality and solutions that were being relied upon in regards to sequencing, which did not exist in a form anything like it at the time for MariaDB. There is a sequencing engine as part of the solution, but it works nothing like the Oracle solution and this had already been considered by Vernon in his initial research into the OSDBMS.

Triggers, love them or hate them, are one of the necessary evils. Vernon's viewpoint was like most DBAs and database programmers in that they have their place, but use them as little as possible and don't overdue it. The alternative can have a very substantial impact on database performance, so part of his approach to the migration was to try to get rid of as many as possible, in particularly those that were not needed and did not make sense. Like many database applications, both the legacy CFW and SFW products used triggers for tracking the history of transactions as the application makes its way through the system. Oracle's built-in optimization capabilities are very robust, so a major concern here was going from a solution like Oracle's to one that did not have some of those same capabilities. The best recommendation in this type of transition is to limit your impact as much as possible from a performance viewpoint, to give the new solution breathing room and yourself headroom to focus on a successful migration instead of dealing with performance issues.

There are some slight differences between Oracle's implementation of database triggers and that of other database vendors, but what we are going to look at here will be specific to those differences in comparison with MariaDB, which are going to be virtually identical to the differences between Oracle and MySQL. The first and most impactful difference is easily observed with the fact that with Oracle one can write a single trigger that will function on multiple possible transactions types, but for MariaDB one must write a separate trigger for each possibility.

Note   MariaDB now supports triggers on multiple transaction types.

Here we will take a look at an Oracle trigger that executes based on either an insert or an update in Listing 3-1 as compared with the same trigger operation ported to MariaDB in Listing 3-2. This is actually not a bad thing, as it forces one to keep the two actions separate instead of having a large amount of code to troubleshoot and read through; it is much easier to debug and code the processes being separate functionality. In essence, it is actually much easier to support and maintain, so one could actually chalk this up to being a benefit, especially if one is coding triggers for large tables with many columns.

Listing 3-1.   Oracle History Trigger

```
CREATE OR REPLACE TRIGGER TRIGGER_NAME
AFTER INSERT OR UPDATE
ON TABLE_NAME
FOR EACH ROW
BEGIN
IF INSERTING
THEN
...DO SOME INSERT WORK;
ELSIF UPDATING
THEN
...DO SOME UPDATE WORK;
END IF;
END;
```

Listing 3-2. Comparable MariaDB Triggers

```
CREATE TRIGGER TRIGGER_NAME_INS
AFTER INSERT ON TABLE_NAME
FOR EACH ROW
BEGIN
...DO SOME INSERT WORK;
END;
CREATE TRIGGER TRIGGER_NAME_UPD
AFTER UPDATE ON TABLE_NAME
FOR EACH ROW
BEGIN
...DO SOME UPDATE WORK;
END;
```

As discussed and one can see here, this lends itself to being a benefit in that the code is broken down into separate components, and this means when migrating from Oracle to MariaDB one has the potential to double their number of triggers that are written in this fashion. Different database administrators will probably look at this in different ways; however, one does view the difference as really a triviality with benefits of organized processing and reduced possibility of human error. Instead of opening one trigger with a magnanimous number of fields being processed that are dependent on multiple manners in which they can be fired (INSERT|UPDATE|DELETE), to troubleshoot only one of the firing processes and possibly making a keystroke error that breaks both portions, one is only working on one aspect at a time.

Note   MariaDB 10.3 introduces temporal tables, making it potentially easier to maintain a history of change over time.

Another crucial bit of Oracle functionality that is highly used is the concept of sequences, and FWP used these in many operations, which MariaDB does not. At least not in the same manner in which Oracle provides sequences and the functions used to manipulate them, so this meant a little ingenuity to provide this functionality to support both the legacy and standardized Financial Widget's code bases. As of this writing MariaDB has since added similar functionality in their latest version 10.3 in 2018, but prior to that it did not exist. This was not a showstopper and turned out to be a simple solution to what might seem a complex problem.

Looking at it from a data and programming logic perspective, an Oracle sequence was essentially a collection of parameter and value-based information related to a named object that had built-in functions to access and manipulate portions of that information. These two functions are NEXTVAL and CURRVAL and they do exactly what it sounds like they would do:

- CURRVAL returns the current value of the sequence

- NEXTVAL increments the sequence by the *increment by* value in the sequence definition and returns that value

Looking at the parameter and value relationship of a sequence as a collection of information lends itself to the idea of field and field values of a table layout, or at least that's how Vernon saw it, so he folded the sequence information into a table in MariaDB and wrote functions to perform the same functionality as Oracle's NEXTVAL and CURRVAL. Figure 3-1 shows the information he used to create the sequence table for this functionality. Then, using this table design, the two routines were written to perform the same functionality that the same Oracle versions did. To be unique and creative, Vernon effectually named them NEXTVAL and CURRVAL.

```
+----------------+---------------------+------+-----+----------------------+-------+
| Field          | Type                | Null | Key | Default              | Extra |
+----------------+---------------------+------+-----+----------------------+-------+
| seq_name       | varchar(50)         | NO   | PRI | NULL                 |       |
| increment_by   | int(10) unsigned    | NO   |     | 1                    |       |
| min_val        | int(10) unsigned    | NO   |     | 1                    |       |
| max_val        | bigint(20) unsigned | NO   |     | 18446744073709551615 |       |
| cur_val        | bigint(20) unsigned | YES  |     | 1                    |       |
| cycle          | tinyint(1)          | NO   |     | 0                    |       |
+----------------+---------------------+------+-----+----------------------+-------+
```

Figure 3-1. *Table layout for the sequencing driver table*

The stored procedures were in Vernon's opinion easier to convert than the triggers that were already done. Like the triggers did, the stored procedures also called Oracle built-ins like sysdate() and systimestamp() were the top contenders here and had to be replaced with *now()* and *current_timestamp()* in order to work in MariaDB. The team at MariaDB had been quoted as saying that more than 90% of Oracle PL SQL would work on MariaDB PL SQL. Vernon was lucky enough to find out that 100% of the stored procedures and functions in use by the databases he managed worked with a few minor changes.

There were some other items in use on the databases such as materialized views for a reporting application; however, the design was very rudimentary, short sighted, and lacked capabilities for useful trend analysis. Vernon had his eye on this for quite some time and did not want it to propagate from the one customer that was using it, predominantly because the views were on a refresh of every 15 minutes in order to provide up to date reporting for the customers. Imagine three views performing a refresh every 15 minutes on 30 databases on the same server that had the following characteristics:

- Refreshed every 15 minutes

- Each contained varying subsets of the same superset.

- All dates and timestamps were being converted to numbers.

- The numbers were then queried against a helper table for querying.

- Multiple data transformations, besides the dates and timestamps

- The query that refreshed and created the views was a conglomeration of archaic, poorly performing joins and subjoins.

Needless to say, this design did not make the cut over to MariaDB and instead it was replaced with a fully functional alternative that could be used to track trend analysis all the way back to when the customer started using the system. This is crucial, especially in the financial sector where long-term and mid-term trend analysis can mean the difference between profit and loss. Having reporting capability that is based on materialized views that are pulling data from tables that are being purged on a routine basis per either contractual obligation or auditing purposes was of limited use. This would be a good example of how not to design a reporting feature on the back end.

Much of the additional legacy code for electronic data warehousing style reports and database management had been written using a lot of shell scripts.

Application Code

Migrating code that had been around for many years and had a lot of Oracle-specific logic, Oracle-specific SQL semantics, and used what are called Oracle built-ins was where the real concern was. After all, for the most part a database is nothing more than a collection of structured data, but talking about code written to access and process that data in a very specific way was where things could get a little nasty. One of the biggest inhibiting factors for many other OSDBMS solutions had to do with the way that they encrypted data, or actually didn't encrypt the data, which meant much of that had to be done at the application and SQL invocation level in order to encrypt the data just before or as it was being entered and then do the same processing when trying to access the data. This would mean significant hours, in some cases possibly years, to accomplish a complete rewrite. FWP was not in the position to afford this both fiscally or time-wise, so just as Vernon had scheduled some time with resources from MariaDB, so did the development team, which also made a huge impact on the migration.

There were a lot of reservations and resistance to the database migration from a developer and architect standpoint, as nobody really wanted to get into what seemed like such a momentous task. Historically the team had to write an in-house set of daemons to maintain stated connections to the Oracle database backend, to alleviate the time and processing involved in making a new connection each time a database transaction was issued. As it turns out these daemons were written in Oracle's Pro*C and during the training Vernon came in to talk with the group about the current MariaDB footprint, at which time a few different things were brought up. When talking about Maxscale and how it worked as a proxy, the in-house written daemons where brought up. This initiated a discussion that ended with a solution that had a far-reaching impact when the trainer stated that those could still be used with a wrapper to do the same job for MariaDB. This opened things up quite a bit and brought about a much more optimistic viewpoint from the entire group in the training session.

The discussion then turned to many more topics such as what the database team planned to do about sequences, because they didn't exist like they did with Oracle. Vernon already not only had the answer for them but had developed and thoroughly tested the solution. It appeared that the excitement was starting to transfer around the room with the capabilities and that, yes, MariaDB was absolutely a viable solution. It seemed as if it instilled a new vigor in the team that was previously dreading having to start the process. All of this occurred in the calendar year of 2016 and no matter the level of excitement to start working with a new database technology, it would be almost a year later to the day of the developer training before an actual customer's development region started hitting a MariaDB database. This nobody's fault, however, but was primarily due to the size of the company and the amount of resources that could be pulled off of other projects and be given the time to start working on the application side of things.

In regard to the database side of this migration, Vernon did not waste any time and had that first customer's database migrated over to MariaDB where it sat unused for almost a year. He also scheduled a week of on-site training for the team of DBAs so that when the application side of things took off, the hope was that everyone would be up to the task. Once the project took off in spring of the following year it really picked up some steam, and by the end of the year approximately 4.5% of 20 million production transactions had rolled through the new database solution. By the end of February of 2018 that ratio of the company's transactions going through the production databases would grow to an astounding 42%. They were making up for lost time.

Becoming Database Agnostic

The aforementioned training session brought about a lot of ideas, as mentioned. The fact that they could slightly modify the Oracle-specific connection state daemons to work with MariaDB was huge. This later led to the novel idea that if they could do this, then why not take it a step further and modify it to the point that upon startup the daemon could ascertain which database solution it was connecting to and process any transactions appropriately. This also pointed them down the path of many other observations.

If they can wrap their daemons with enough code that it would know what type of database it was connecting to and process in a befitting manner, then this could be done for virtually any other database solution.

This meant that they could move to the realm of having their application become database agnostic and never be so engrained in a solution as they had become with Oracle over the years. They were and are still hoping that MariaDB will become a mainstay in their product line, but anything can happen and generally will.

All of this work towards becoming database agnostic and the fact they could use the same connection state daemons also led Vernon to an additional idea on leveraging this to help move existing customers from Oracle to MariaDB with little or no impact via parallel writes. In essence this meant that an application server could be running two different daemons strictly for database writes. One daemon would handle normal transaction processing to the Oracle database while another daemon could send all write transactions in duplicate to the MariaDB until such time all transactions could be routed solely to the MariaDB version.

Historically, any time Vernon had to move data from one Oracle database version to another it always meant a big portion of down-time, but with this idea it meant that they could pick a cut-off point and thus the down-time and transition could be minimalized to the extreme. Database migrations were always tricky, but to be able to do it with almost no down-time, now that would be novel. The process broke down like this:

- Analyze the customer's workflow to find the optimum number of days that they ever went back to on an application.

  - For instance, 90 days

- Pick a starting date and begin the parallel write process.

- In the meantime all normal work is flowing through the Oracle side, while all writes are going to both.

- Once the 90-day mark is hit, "flip the switch" to have all transactions start going to MariaDB.

- While the customer continues processing with MariaDB, all the data out past one's 90-day time frame can then be migrated without any service interruption.

  - This could also be done during the 90-day parallel write period as long as none of the older data was changed.

The biggest takeaway from FWP and what many in the company would certainly recommend was to engage the MariaDB teams and leverage them to get off the ground and running. They found it to be crucial to their success in making this transition, and as well it had the added benefit in regard to idea and process generation throughout and after the engagements.

This only covers a few options and ideas to make a change like this, more specifically ones that fit the business needs of a small company. A bigger company or global corporation could throw a lot more resources and staff at a project like this, which opens up many more possibilities. For Vernon and the rest of the team at FWP, the approaches outlined here worked the best for their situation. It is recommended to do one's own research and explore solutions that fit the individual situation, as there are so many tools, utilities, and database migration solutions out there that may fit their need.

Moving forward with MariaDB for the team was absolutely solidified at this point in time, with a few caveats that would need to be addressed from the database side programming. At this point it was also a good time to start analyzing existing solutions that could be improved during the database migration. This analysis would coincide perfectly with moving into the more technical aspects of migrating from Oracle to MariaDB. The two topics are complimentary to a successful migration as change is inevitable.

CHAPTER 4

Making the Decision

This chapter will take us through a summary of the Financial Widgets Plus (FWP) team's work and culminate with a sample project definition with an executive summary for the team's presentation in regard to choosing MariaDB as the new DBMS over their existing solution. Even though the raw presentation of the work completed so far speaks for itself, one may find that bringing this all together in a professionally formatted presentation should be the primary goal for any project, much less one with the far-reaching scope of migrating to a completely new database backend for a company's premier product. As with any good analysis it isn't just about presenting the benefits, but also identifying risks and mitigations in order to minimize those risks, along with an overall Cost Benefit Analysis (CBA), and that was Vernon's approach.

The first thing Vernon wanted to address in the decision making was why FWP would want to undertake such a huge project. Why would any entity take on the additional workload? Why would they allocate resources to such a monumental task when they might be used elsewhere? Why shouldn't they just stay on their legacy system and continue with business as usual? Ultimately, all of these questions can be answered by the cost analysis phase of this project when it comes to presenting the benefits; however, he also wanted to present a path for moving forward and completing it successfully with a systematically planned approach. A strategy for success if you will that should include the benefits, cost analysis, and at a minimum the first phase of the implementation.

Extolling the Benefits

The benefits of MariaDB over the existing solution employed by FWP were not easily overlooked and Vernon could not see any reason to not proceed further; however, that final decision would be up to the head of the company and ultimately ownership. There were still questions to be answered and risks to be identified in regard to such a monumental change as performing a complete overhaul of their application's backend. When we talk about extolling the benefits, we want to effectively answer all off the questions as to why this change should be considered and the reasons the work is beneficial.

Part of any good solution analysis begins with identifying the problem and scope along with weighing the benefits of change to the entity. Those benefits can range broadly and should present a solution to a beneficial business need that contains a positive Return on Investment (ROI) to the company. Cost savings can be in time and resources or just an overall existing process improvement of deploying a new solution, altering an existing solution, and identifying the drivers that make the engagement successful.

The benefits for the MariaDB solution as compared with the existing solution were substantial and culminated in a list that could extend for many pages. What we will do here is provide a synopsis of benefits that were considered to be the top purveyors of change:

- Costs
  - Overall Software Licensing and Support costs savings as well as being hardware and virtualization agnostic
  - Driving the bottom line, allowing the company to invest savings into marketing, staff, and resources and therefore growing their business

- Secure

  - Fulfils security requirements for data at rest and in transit

- Scalable

  - Scalable to meet growing business needs and reduced licensing complexity means less drain on staff.

- High Availability

  - Leveraging Enterprise Clustering with Galera and Maxscale

  - Location failover capabilities with hybrid replication deployments

Presenting Cost Savings

It does not make sense for a company to begin a project that does not benefit them in some way, and Vernon knew that with the MariaDB solution the cost savings and ROI were going to be huge, so huge to the point that everything else might be considered inconsequential. In fact, the costs savings alone when projected over time were enough to offset virtually any risks involved as well as the costs in allocating the workforce necessary to complete the task. Essentially, by looking at costs in their most simplified classifications of Indirect Costs and Direct Costs, Vernon was able to present a very thorough analysis to the company. There were many different nuances when it came to attempting to arrive at a solid foundation for a CBA such as price changes due to vendor-experienced Costs of Doing Business (CODB) increases, defining and identifying cost types, and bringing it all together into a well-organized and documented project scope of work.

When it came time to present findings to the upper management level at FWP, Vernon knew the numbers would speak for themselves when compared with the current impact to their overhead and ultimately the bottom line when looking at the amount of money that had been spent over the years in licensing and support fees on their current DBMS solution. The team had also witnessed price increases over the years with their current solution, and as with any product or service in the tech industry it is virtually unheard of for the costs to decrease over time. These price increases are generally based on a percentage of existing costs that can be accounted for in projections, so if one compares a projected increase on 1.2 million dollars versus 400 thousand dollars at similar rates, then there is even further argument for change.

Looking at any project from a cost perspective they can always be simplified down into two essential classifications: Direct Costs and Indirect Costs. These can change depending upon the point of analysis, so for instance from Vernon's standpoint his Direct and Indirect Costs for the database team could be different than those of another team within the same organization, for instance the development team. For this project, due to the scope being virtually company wide, Vernon chose to look at it from a broader scope as compared to the perspective of solely his team alone.

In identifying the Direct Costs for the database solution change, Vernon was able to come up with the following items as being what he considered the primary candidates related to the project:

- Software Licensing and Support
    - DBMS Licensing
    - Operating System Licensing
- Database team resources
    - Training on new DBMS
    - Database side programming development, porting, and testing

- Increased role in management of DBMS' although costly, their existing solution has many built-in capabilities for optimization, so a more hands-on approach will be required for monitoring, tuning, and performance evaluations.

  - Phasing out the legacy DBMS

  - Migration of existing customers

  - Staff increase will be necessary to meet these needs.

- Development team resources

  - Training for development work with new DBMS

  - Migration of existing customers

  - Application code side development, porting, and testing for DBMS change

Moving on to identifying the Indirect Costs that could be associated with the project:

- Hardware

  - Taking advantage of updated server architecture

- Systems team resources

  - Deploying and maintaining server OS and hardware

- Quality Analysis

  - Increased QA load for regression testing

- Security

  - Development and deployment of new security testing and utilities oriented towards the new DBMS

One can now start to really appreciate the scope, the amount of work, the resource allocation demands, and the time that will be required in the migration to a new database solution for the team at FWP. This is also why the development and documentation of a full analysis and scope of work is crucial. Being as thorough as possible with leaving no stones unturned as well as knowing which stones one can minimize, and in some cases ignore, successfully can mean the difference in the failure and completion of a project, especially one as large as migrating to a new DBMS.

Without a detailed analysis and thorough understanding of the requirements for a project, one cannot count on successful completion as an end result; however, that is only part of making a change like this successfully. Vernon knew this just as much as he knew that they had to also develop a game plan with a winning strategy to really make this happen. After all we are talking about a set of core products that are leveraged heavily by institutions in the financial industry, where a mistake could very well result in catastrophic implications for FWP as well as their respective customers. That is a heavy burden and a lot of responsibility that could be a career ending situation, not to mention business ending. So now it was time to analyze how they were going to make this happen in a manner that gets them on the new platform while lowering risk and mitigating potential problems.

Develop a Strategy

With the benefits and cost effectiveness barriers out of the way, it was time to have an initial strategy for the implementation of the new database solution—what many would refer to as Phase 1 of the implementation. What Vernon wanted to accomplish with his strategy here was to develop a road map that would take FWP from having no existing MariaDB infrastructure or footprint whatsoever in their data center to having the new database solution deployed. This deployment would be followed with getting a customer's data migrated over and their application widgets taking full advantage of the new DBMS, ultimately resulting in it all eventually migrating out to a full production level implementation.

Vernon and the team had surmised that it did not make a lot of sense to make a huge investment in hardware and other resources until they had an environment up and running to validate that MariaDB was in fact the solution they had been looking for. In the meantime, it was decided to keep the deployment simple and as cost effective as possible, the KISS (Keep It Simple, Stupid) design principle being still as relevant today as when it was first phrased. This would help to lower the risk on the off chance that the solution turned out to not be a good fit for their application.

The initial MariaDB deployment would turn out to be very cost effective in that FWP had recently gone through a hardware refresh and thus had several HP Proliant DL380 G7 servers that could be repurposed to provide the initial hardware to house the MariaDB database deployments. These were old and outdated servers; however, they had the memory capabilities and processing power to serve out their usefulness as supplying the proof of concept for the new database solution.

Sticking with the principle of KISS, Vernon made the executive decision to keep the first MariaDB deployment simple as well. He chose to stick with single, stand-alone nodes to house the database solution using Maxscale and MariaDB Replication to provide replicated failover for the first incarnation. These standalone nodes would run on the G7 server architecture; however, for the purpose of providing the Maxscale footprint, seeing how it was such a lightweight solution, Vernon decided that it would be perfectly suited to virtualized environments.

With many existing customers already on the legacy solution, it seemed that the best-case scenario would be to analyze the existing customers for an initial candidate. A meeting was scheduled that included representatives from the different teams to assist in this portion, as with many of the legacy customers only the most recent adhered to any type of standardization or common code base. What the team was looking for was a candidate that would be lightweight in regard to data retention, which would mean less data to migrate, and that would involve minimal code changes in order to point them to the new database solution. This turned out to be a pretty quick and simple job, as all teams were in agreement when the requirements were discussed in that one customer stood out above all the rest. This customer was lightweight, maintained a small data footprint due to retention policies, and FWP provided more of a Software as a Service (SAAS) than any other customer.

With the hardware lined out and a first candidate for migration designated, FWP started to move forward at a rapid pace with the MariaDB solution. Although, others might choose a different path or even be migrating with completely different database solutions, the lessons learned here are applicable to virtually any project when success is the ultimate goal. There are some good lessons here, and when one combines this with the fact that Vernon lead the team through a successful migration from one database technology to another, the roadmap he developed is valid and applicable for others to use as a basis in their own work, and the same methodologies are adaptable to other types of large-scale projects.

Putting it Together

After detailed documentation of the benefits, cost analysis, and development of an implementation strategy, the next step is putting this all into a nicely formatted project documentation for presentation and approval. There are many acceptable preformatted project document outlines readily available, many are free and easily downloadable, and all will work. You can even make up your own; however, there are a few minimum sections that one should include in their project documentation. What we will present here are the requirements that Vernon used as a format for his documentation.

At a minimum, one will want to have a well-organized document that contains specific requirements in an easily readable format that begins with an Executive Summary. This can and will be the most important part of your document and should be treated as such, as the target of this summary will be the company leaders at the highest level who will have the final say on your project. One does not want to get too wordy and should stick to the facts related to the most important portions of your project and what benefit they will provide to the business. This first section will be the difference on whether your reader stops and moves on to something else, setting your project aside, or continues to digest your document in its entirety with a much higher potential of getting the go ahead. If you have spent the time to get to that point, spend the time and make the Executive Summary pop, otherwise you are wasting your time as well as your reader's time.

The Executive Summary is where you grab the reader's attention and effactually sell your project, enticing the target audience to read the rest of the document for a more detailed breakdown of the work. This does not mean that one skimps on the remaining document, as the details are just as important and if you don't have the specifics to back up the Executive Summary, your project can end up dead in the water as well.

The benefits of MariaDB over Oracle from a pricing and side by side comparison did not require too much on the project presentation side, as it pretty much spoke for itself. With many utilities and capabilities that come prepackaged with MariaDB it seems that Oracle is going to have some very capable competition in the secure database market. It satisfies auditing requirements, is scalable, and cost effective—with the latter being something that Oracle currently cannot compete with. The one thing to glean from the analysis as presented over these first few chapters is that although MariaDB is a very cost-effective solution from a support and licensing viewpoint, the only downside is that it will require more hands on from one's database administration team. Even with the additional staffing needs, Oracle is effactually blown out of the water by what MariaDB has to offer.

CHAPTER 5

MariaDB Solution

As discussed in Chapter 4 in regard to the initial deployment of their MariaDB solution at Financial Widgets Plus (FWP) and keeping with the KISS principle, the team chose to stand up a stand-alone environment with replication. Using this as the basis for their proof of concept work turned out to enable them to get an active MariaDB environment deployed quickly and easily in order to validate what they had already perceived as a viable solution to their database solution alternative. Once the proof of concept was complete, the team then went on to deploy a much more robust high availability solution. Here we will get into detail on the setup and deployments as completed by Vernon's team, to get them familiar with the database solution by enabling them to rapidly deploy and then extend their MariaDB footprint.

Starting with a stand-alone install of the MariaDB database solution provided them a vehicle to prove their concepts and initial evaluation with a simple setup. The team then went on to evaluate Replication and ultimately to a full blown Galera Cluster. The use of a phased approach in their implementation minimized risk as well as allowing the team to increase their knowledge of the system from the basic setup to the much more advanced deployment. This approach was also tantamount to the project's success, as they were able to maintain a simplified footprint for development and testing work while working on the more advanced solutions. This allowed for continuous integration and improvement throughout the migration process without interruption of the day to day operations.

© William Wood 2019
W. Wood, *Migrating to MariaDB*, https://doi.org/10.1007/978-1-4842-3997-1_5

The team at FWP had migrated from the financial sector staple of HP-UX many years ago and had updated to RedHat Enterprise Linux (RHEL) as their companywide server class operating system. Therefore, all installation and configuration errata will be based on RHEL as the operating system of choice, which for completeness it should be noted that it is packaged with CentOS. One can easily apply the same database system setup and configurations across virtually any Linux distribution of choice. RedHat being an open source and community driven commercial variation of the Linux operating system also has a community release called Fedora that could be used freely in one's proof of concept work in a sandbox environment. The only differences might be with the installation of the MariaDB libraries and code base as to whether one's distributions leverage installation utilities such as yum, rpm, apt-get, and so on. Since we will be installing and configuring MariaDB software on RHEL version 7, the following documentation will be oriented towards that distribution and its libraries and utilities.

Preinstallation Considerations

The setup, configuration, and deployment of the MariaDB solution by Vernon's team, although kept in their simplest form, required some consideration. Being new to the technology and not knowing how well the database would perform with their application code meant some guesswork would be involved as to system requirements. MariaDB leverages the Linux temporary directory and would require enough space to perform operations. In order to fully test the new database solution, encryption for data in transit and data at rest also must be deployed along with the installation.

Using the system deployments of the Oracle RAC nodes seemed to be a good starting point for overall system requirements as far as system memory allocation and CPU. The changes that were made were in regard to allocating specific disk mounts for MariaDB use. This would allow them to size and resize the mounts arbitrarily of other system and application processes, with the added benefit that if something went wrong on the database side it would not bring down the entire system. These decisions regarding disk space were to provide the database its own mount point for data files, logs, etc. as compared with the default location as well as its own temporary file mount.

One of the primary requirements in the search for a new database solution for the team at FWP was the capability for the encryption of data, both for data at rest and data in transit, so this had to be a part of the testing and evaluation sandbox. The encryption of data in transit has been around with MySQL for quite some time with the use of SSL and requiring connections to use SSL; however, the advent of the encryption of data at rest beginning with MariaDB 10.1 was new, so it had to be set up and evaluated.

Note   MariaDB actually supports an updated form of SSL known as TLS. However, it is common for the term SSL to still be used even though TLS is the intended meaning.

The installation of the MariaDB software as well as many of the lower level configuration settings does require root level system access. From the FWP perspective, much of the system setup, mounting of storage, and various other operations are handled by their group of system administrators. In most cases, from a business and security viewpoint this will be similar due to separation of duty constraints for most businesses handling secure data. Our focal point here will be primarily from the database administrator side for the setup and configurations, but anything of particular mention will be notated for the reader.

MariaDB Stand-Alone with Replication

Starting with MariaDB as a stand-alone database server is the perfect place to gain experience and find out how your database driven application is going to work. It can be set up on a rapidly deployed virtualized environment that is low cost and low impact to your systems team and will get you up and running quickly. The files are easily downloaded directly from the MariaDB website, which is how this exercise will be approached, and are also available in most vendors' code repositories and can be pulled into one's internal repository in order to be more readily available.

Note   Be very prudent if your company maintains its own repository for yum or apt-get based installations and updates. It is highly recommended that all database software updates should be done in a controlled manner and should not coincide with operating system updates,; if your operating system updates automatically pull from an internal repository, then your database software could be at risk of an unplanned update.

The MariaDB code repository contains installation files for the following operating systems:

- WINDOWS

- REDHAT / CENTOS

- DEBIAN

- UBUNTO

- SLES

The files required for an installation of a MariaDB release are all packaged together into a large tar file and must be unpacked prior to installation; however, we can also take a sneak peek by passing specific parameters to the tar command to see that there are a lot of files (Listing 5-1 and Listing 5-2). Once the tar archive is unpacked for a base install, there are only a few of the rpm files that will be required for the base installation:

- MariaDB-10.2.15-centos73-x86_64-server.rpm

- MariaDB-10.2.15-centos73-x86_64-client.rpm

- MariaDB-10.2.15-centos73-x86_64-common.rpm

- MariaDB-10.2.15-centos73-x86_64-shared.rpm

Listing 5-1. Using the tar Command to List the Archive Contents

```
# tar -tvf mariadb-10.2.15-rhel-7-x86_64-rpms.tar
```

Listing 5-2. Using the tar Command to Extract the Contents

```
# tar -xvf mariadb-10.2.15-rhel-7-x86_64-rpms.tar
```

Note   This is a little confusing and it should be noted that the tar file will contain the designation of RHEL, and when unpacked it will create a directory designated RHE. However, the individual install files will have the designation of CENTOS. Both Linux distributions use the exact same files, so the naming construct although confusing has no deleterious effect.

The installation of the MariaDB software is made easy with the yum installation and update utility; see Listing 5-3 for a single line command to install all 4 packages. As mentioned previously, one must be very careful if including database packages in their own local repository, as the application of an unplanned patching event can be catastrophic if not done in a controlled environment. The author's own recommendation is to always keep system updates disjoint and performed at different times than database updates for a very valid and significant reason. It is extraordinarily difficult to troubleshoot failures when you have patched both your database and your operating system at the same time. Which patch broke everything is not always easily definable, and the last thing you want is people from different groups standing around pointing the finger at each other while your customers are experiencing a prolonged and potentially unplanned outage. Play it safe to plan and perform your deployment's maintenance accordingly.

Listing 5-3. Using yum to Install the Required MariaDB Packages

```
# yum install MariaDB-10.2.15-centos73-x86_64-server.rpm
MariaDB-10.2.15-centos73-x86_64-client.rpm MariaDB-10.2.15-
centos73-x86_64-shared.rpm MariaDB-10.2.15-centos73-x86_64-
common.rpm
```

The base install will put everything into the default locations along with placing some sample configuration files on your system for MariaDB to use on database start up. We do not want to start the database up at this time; instead we want to start our configuration of the system in order to have everything in place at startup. A few things to note about the base install:

- Default location for configuration files

  - /etc/my.cnf.d

- Default location for database files and log files

  - /var/lib/mysql

Since we will be using encryption, that will be the next step in our setup and although we can put those files virtually anywhere, the default location was chosen for consistency. For data in transit our deployment will be using Secure Socket Layer (SSL), so the keys will have to be created in order to take advantage of the network security layer it provides. This key creation process is described in Listing 5-4 and since they will be created in the default location, the first step would be to move to that directory so the files will then be created within the target location.

Listing 5-4. Creating SSL Encryption Keys for Data in Transit

```
# cd /var/lib/mysql

# openssl genrsa 2048 > ca-key.pem

# openssl req -new -x509 -nodes -days 3600 -key ca-key.pem -out
  ca-cert.pem

# openssl req -newkey rsa:2048 -days 3600 -nodes -keyout
  server-key.pem -out server-req.pem

# openssl rsa -in server-key.pem -out server-key.pem

# openssl x509 -req -in server-req.pem -days 3600 -CA ca-cert.
  pem -CAkey cakey.pem -set_serial 01 -out server-cert.pem

# openssl req -newkey rsa:2048 -days 3600 -nodes -keyout
  client-key.pem -out client-req.pem

# openssl rsa -in client-key.pem -out client-key.pem

# openssl x509 -req -in client-req.pem -days 3600 -CA ca-cert.
  pem -CAkey cakey.pem -set_serial 01 -out client-cert.pem

# openssl verify -CAfile ca.pem server-cert.pem client-cert.pem
```

Note   It is highly recommended to create backup copies of all encryption related files and keys—local for quick access in an emergency, as well as remotely in case of a full Disaster Recovery situation.

The next phase is creating the encryption keys for the security of our data at rest by encrypting all data that is considered PII or PCI scoped. This will also take advantage of the openssl libraries in order to create the initial keys that will be used to encrypt the tables that contain the data that is targeted as requiring a high level of protection. When compared to the creation of the keys for data protection at the network layer, the process is much easier for the data at rest in that it is a single command that will generate the output that can then be placed in your key file. For simplicity sake we will name this file keys.txt with read access protection. The creation process is covered in Listing 5-5.

Listing 5-5. Creating Encryption Keys for Data at Rest

```
# openssl enc -aes-256-ctr -k mypass -P  -md sha1
```

With the data encryption portion of the setup complete, the next steps will be the configuration of the database server as well as the client. As previously mentioned, these files are located in the default location of /etc/my.cnf.d, so this will be our next focal point in the setup and deployment process. The installation of MariaDB will create default configuration files for the database; these are very rudimentary and sometimes will require significant customization throughout the lifetime of a deployment. These configuration files consist of a file for the database server as well as one for the client, and are easily identified due to their naming convention:

- Server configuration file: /etc/my.cnf.d/server.cnf

- Client configuration file: /etc/my.cnf.d/client.cnf

Continuing in the same order as the creation of the keys, the first step will be to configure the local client configuration for encrypted communications. Essentially we are pointing the client to the location of the SSL files for use in connection initiation with the server, which is accomplished by adding the file names and paths to the client.cnf file, as shown in Listing 5-6. The server must also be configured to use the server side SSL files in order to communicate with the client, so a similar entry must be made in the server.cnf file (Listing 5-7).

Listing 5-6. Client Configuration File Rntry for Use of SSL

```
[client]
ssl-cert = /var/lib/mysql/client-cert.pem
ssl-key  = /var/lib/mysql/client-key.pem
```

This completes the configuration requirements for the network encryption of data in transit and is all the editing required for the client configuration file. The SSL configuration on the server side resides within the server.cnf and doesn't have to be in any particular location or order; however, it does have to be included in order to use SSL encryption of the database communications.

Note   When patching and applying updates to your database the configuration files can and will be overwritten. It is generally good practice to maintain a backup of both files on a remote server, as well to add the step of creating a copy of your configuration files locally prior to any changes.

Listing 5-7. Server Configuration File Entry for Use of SSL

```
[mysqld]
# SSL settings
ssl-ca   = /var/lib/mysql/ca-cert.pem
ssl-cert = /var/lib/mysql/server-cert.pem
ssl-key  = /var/lib/mysql/server-key.pem
```

This completes the encryption setup portion and allows us to move along to the rest of the server configuration, which gets a little more involved. The server configuration file can go from the short and simple to an exceedingly complex, hard to follow, and lengthy array of server parameter value combinations. Therefore, the best approach is to start with a well-organized file and build upon that organizational standard as one's needs and requirements evolve over time along with the deployment. This is exactly how this will be approached with the sample configuration settings that will be shared here in the example server configuration file provided, beginning with standard configuration settings in Listing 5-8.

Listing 5-8. Server Configuration File General Settings

```
[mysqld]
# turn on the performance schema
performance_schema=ON
# General
basedir                 = /usr
datadir                 = /data_mount/mysql
tmpdir                  = /tmp_mount/tmp
report_host             = sandbox1
port                    = 3306
user                    = mysql
character-set-server    = utf8
collation-server        = utf8_general_ci
optimizer_switch        = 'index_merge=on,index_
                          merge_union=on,index_merge_
                          sort_union=on,index_merge_
                          intersection=on,index_merge_sort_
                          intersection=off,index_condition_
                          pushdown=on,derived_merge=on,derived_
                          with_keys=on,firstmatch=on,loo
                          sescan=on,materialization=on,
                          in_to_exists=on,semijoin=on,partial_
                          match_rowid_merge=on,partial_
                          match_table_scan=on,subquery_
                          cache=on,mrr=on,mrr_cost_based=on,mrr_
                          sort_keys=off,outer_join_with_
```

```
                          cache=on,semijoin_with_cache=on,join_
                          cache_incremental=on,join_cache_
                          hashed=on,join_cache_bka=on,optimize_
                          join_buffer_size=on,table_
                          elimination=on,extended_keys=on'
event_scheduler          = ON
log_error                = sandbox.err
log_warnings             = 1
```

Replication Limits and Testing

At the time of this project there were some limitations with stand-alone replication in a master-slave scenario in regard to high availability and failover, which could be overcome with some work. That capability is now available within Maxscale using GTID (Global Transaction ID) and if the automatic rejoin is enabled if the master is lost and recovers it will automatically reconfigure as a slave.

Testing the replication features was completed both locally and to a remote data center across the country. This was one of the simpler features of MariaDB to test; however, one should test the replication of both data and structure. This is where Vernon and his team ran into an interesting anomaly with using the create or replace functionality for triggers, stored procedures, and functions. These objects do not replicate successfully, and one must explicitly drop the objects and recreate them. This is by no means a showstopper, but it does have some implications for making changes on the fly.

Galera Clustering

Once replication failover was tested, the next phase was to evaluate MariaDB with Galera Clustering. The replication setup provided a quick and simple deployment to get MariaDB up and running in the datacenter at FWP. It also provided an environment for their development team to start their portion of the work in migrating the company's software to the new DBMS. The company required full failover capabilities just like what they had with Oracle RAC, to alleviate downtime and service interruptions. A Galera cluster was the next step with a minimum three-node deployment.

The Galera software rpm is included in the same distribution files as the base release, and the setup requires a few changes to the server configuration file. The settings shown in Listing 5-9 are the minimum run time settings required to for a cluster setup. The naming constructs and parameters are straightforward, with wsrep_node_address being the IP address of the server configuration files node and wsrep_cluster_address being the list of all cluster members.

Listing 5-9. Server Configuration File Galera Settings

```
[galera]
wsrep_on=ON
wsrep_data_home_dir=/<path>/galera
wsrep_node_address=<node_ip>
wsrep_provider=/usr/lib64/galera/libgalera_smm.so
wsrep_cluster_address="gcomm://<ip_1>,<ip_2>,<ip_3>"
wsrep_cluster_name="<some_cluster_name>"
```

The configuration settings should be the same across all nodes except for the individual node address, and a distinct cluster name should be assigned to each cluster as deployed. Once the first node is up and operational one can then move on to the second node in the cluster. with the understanding that the second node will then synchronize with the first node. An observation here is that the time it takes to synchronize will be heavily dependent on the number of databases and their size. Initial setup should not take any time; however this time will increase as more databases and data are added. Another item worth noting is that in most cases a new node joining the cluster will get syncrhonized with the most up to date node; this is generally the current Master node. This will cause a failover event, as the Master will go into a quiesced state to transfer data to the joining node and a new Master will be chosen unless a specific donor node is designated. If the Master is the only node in the cluster when a node attempts to join, there will be a loss of service because the Master will still go into a quiescing state and will accept no transactions until it is done bringing the new node up to state.

Some things to note about differences between Oracle RAC and Galera Clustering:

- Oracle RAC is shared disk; Galera is not.

- Oracle RAC has load balancing capabilities; Galera does not.

- Galera has read/write splitting with Maxscale.

- Galera cluster requires a minimum of three nodes.

The Galera Clustering solution does have a few caveats that one must become familiar with in order to support it. The failover capabilities are instantaneous and with Maxscale providing connection routing, stated connections failover seemlessly without issue. If one's application allows for it, read/write splitting with Maxscale can also provide some load balancing capabilities by moving read transactions across the nodes. The biggest impact that Oracle RAC has over Galera is that it supports shared disk via ASM, which reduces network storage overhead for RAC. With Galera the disk requirements are such that each node must have the same amount of disk space allocated because they are all equal copies of one another. With the reduction in overhead of newer storage technologies, this is also not a showstopper.

CHAPTER 6

Change as a Catalyst

When Vernon was first presented with the mandate to start researching alternative database solutions for Financial Widgets Plus (FWP) he saw a much larger opportunity at hand. Coming in to a new company that had a database department that consisted entirely of a group of what he termed as Reactive Database Administrators that had created and deployed an amalgamation of one off solutions and had never explored the concept of standardization, he realized that this was the best thing that could happen to not only FWP, but also to the department that he was now heading up. Where others saw the migration to a new database solution as an opportunity to lower costs significantly and be done with what they perceived as a predatory vendor, Vernon saw this is an opportunity to fix many headaches and problems that had been plaguing the organization for quite some time.

From the very first discussion on the topic he realized that he was going to seize upon this opportunity and use it as a catalyst for change for his department as well as the organization. He had already made some inroads into change once he had taken over the database department with developing and promoting standardization in a few areas. However, this would allow for the opportunity to effect change on an even greater level with the opportunity to rework and fix many of the legacy headaches that plagued his team, and in some ways the entire organization as a whole, with difficult to support and maintain products and services. There were many hours of time spent in the support and maintenance of poorly written and designed database side processes and code. Although some

© William Wood 2019
W. Wood, *Migrating to MariaDB*, https://doi.org/10.1007/978-1-4842-3997-1_6

of that time was in fact billable to the end customers, it was in fact lost time for the organization itself. It was time that was better served being expended working on new and improved solutions, new product lines, and normal maintenance that was sometimes being deferred due to the lack of staffing resources or the time to actually allocate to them.

Up to the point of entertaining a new DBMS solution, Vernon had systematically been pinpointing areas of improvement that could be targeted without major overhauls to the solution side, and the biggest problem was breaching the reactive attitude of the department that he had inherited. This was not just internal to his department, but was also a problem with the way that every other internal team within the organization treated and worked with the database team. He had great disdain for any organization or team being predominantly reactive in nature because it was never conducive to productivity and never provided a positive experience, especially when it was something that could be easily automated or monitored. Of course if there is an outage of some type there is no other approach than to react to the situation, but when the culture is one where the staff is surfing the Internet, shopping, and not maintaining their systems and the end result was a production level outage for a customer, being reactive is not the answer. The first step was to begin promoting a proactive approach for the group of database administrators, which then would begin to flow over and hopefully have the desired impact on the other teams.

The changing of a culture from one of being predominantly reactive to that of taking on a more proactive role and attitude was the largest hurdle that in many ways prepared the database team for the future of migrating to a new database solution. Although it was unknown at the time when Vernon started this arduous task, in self-reflection without crossing this hurdle the team would not have been prepared to take on the level of work involved with migrating from a DBMS such as Oracle's Enterprise Edition (that had the internal optimization capabilities, built in features, and performance utilities that quite simply worked out of the box) to something entirely different like MariaDB. This outlook in no way minimizes the capabilities of the MariaDB solution, but more so maximizes the fact that it does require more hands on, a shift in learning, and ultimately a team of Proactive Database Administrators to manage and support it.

By the time the database team at FWP began working on the MariaDB implementation, this cultural shift was well underway and his own team was becoming much more agile with adopting his more proactive approach in their work and daily duties. This allowed Vernon's team to jump ahead of the project proactively in order to start identifying items that could be improved, the adoption of further standards, and the overall improvement of tasks and services from the database side for the company's offerings.

Evaluating Solutions for Rework

Entering into a change with ramifications such as changing one's DBMS for a complete backend overhaul is a huge undertaking and no stone should be left unturned in outlining the requirements and scope. This includes existing solutions and services that might be outdated, poorly written or could use improvement, and may very well cause a performance impact to your new DBMS. As if migrating to a completely different database weren't enough, one cannot overlook potential performance impacts that lie just outside getting the primary application up and running with the new database solution, which increases the overall scope of the project, furthering the potential for success.

The methodology being introduced here is not new and the largest mitigating factor in a change like this is to not fall prey to tunnel vision but instead to try to be thorough in the analysis of any change requirement across the full scope of the solution. Most software applications that leverage a database-driven backend for transactional application processing do not stop at providing that service and that service alone. There are many other secondary and tertiary services, and beyond, that the database portion of solutions is saddled with. These also need to fall under the microscope because they have the potential to affect one's project. This may be as simple as some daily generated reporting services or as complex as feeding a data warehousing solution designed as a system of record.

Solutions that fall outside the scope of standard transactional processing that were designed and written for a solution like Oracle's Enterprise Edition DBMS in most cases are not going to perform the same against a different database solution. As mentioned, the Oracle database has optimization capabilities that others do not and can make poorly written code or poorly designed objects perform without noticeable issues. The time to find out about these hidden gems is not after everything has been ported and you are up and running in a production environment. Although, from experience there are going to be items at the application code side that undoubtedly will have less than desirable effects, the idea is to mitigate these items to as few, small, and far between as is humanly possible by looking at the bigger picture.

The approach as taken by the database team at FWP was just such an exercise as this. Processes and systems were analyzed that were easily identifiable from the database side thoroughly, in order to evaluate them for potential impact and then addressed systematically. They used the database solution migrations as an opportunity to fix issues with legacy solutions, to adopt standards, and to improve processes and automated solutions. This not only helped to mitigate post migration problems, but also to target solutions that had been developed a long time ago in order to improve them and thus provide a more stable and robust solution to their customers.

Fixing the Legacy

Everyone has been there at some point in their career, where they have been tasked with supporting and maintaining legacy solutions that sometimes turn out to be the bane of their existence. These solutions often turn into considerable time sinks that adversely affect day to day operations and inhibit forward progress in other areas. Sometimes these solutions were written by technical resources that are no longer available and have moved on in some capacity. However, one also sometimes has the distinct pleasure of running across something they did earlier in their career that also offers the same amount of enjoyment. Either way, if you are performing a migration such as this, you are aware of all of these potential targets already and should take advantage of this opportunity to correct these potential time wasters and productivity hurting problems.

The database team at FWP took many of these things into account in their transition, as there were several opportunities for improved level of service. For them, since their company was relatively small and lacked resources to start tackling items on the code side right away, they had the luxury of time on their side to spend evaluating legacy code and processes as targets for improvement. Some of the tasks they chose to tackle were actually redesigned and developed into more robust solutions to the point that no legacy code existed in the migrated solution.

There were many processes that had absolutely no logging or error checking, which meant many times the database team would get notified by other teams, sometimes even customers, that something had failed. Vernon had started to ferret out these lackluster solutions on the Oracle side and augment the existing code to include some levels of logging and error checking, but did not have the time or resources to allocate to them at the level they really required. The transition to the MariaDB solution provided his entire team the ability to address many issues that had been plaguing them as a team, and FWP as a company. They were able to make these changes as part of the migration and move to a more robust, time-saving, and maintainable day to day operational efficiency.

From the database code side, the migration to a new database solution is a great time to evaluate and potentially resolve many of the legacy issues that tend to cause a negative impact. In Vernon's case, going from Oracle to MariaDB provided a great vehicle for this. Even though much of the database side coding would only require slight changes and recoding work due to MariaDB's support for PL/SQL, there are still many built-in functions being leveraged that Oracle has that no other solution has. The fact that much of the database programming code would need to be gone through validated the argument for addressing shortcomings and improving the code base. This may not be true for everyone, but the opportunity should not be passed up for the evaluation and improvement of legacy code and processes.

Standards Adoption

One of the biggest time sinks for Vernon and the team of database administrators at FWP was the lack of standards adoption across the entire organization. For the database team it meant supporting many databases that were largely disjoint in every way possible, but the same policies existed across the entire development team as well. Within a short time of his initial employment, he quickly concluded that nobody historically ever did the same thing the same way twice even when it was the same person performing the work. Vernon set about enacting policies and pushing standardization within his team with the strategy that the avenue he was taking would filter out and have a beneficial side effect across the organization. It was sorely needed and was not going to be an easy task by any account with many bumps and bruises—again the process of database solution migration to the rescue inducing more needed changes.

The problems were so bad that the organization was literally hemorrhaging losses in hours, productivity, and ultimately affecting the bottom line because of it; however, pointing this out would certainly win no political races. The benefits of standards adoption are magnanimously positive, just as the lack of standards is negative. The turnaround times for supporting issues are quite lengthy when standardization methods are not followed in any way, shape, or form, especially if the person familiar with the implementation is not immediately available. Some organizations may be better off, and yet some may be one on even worse footing. However, any reason for the adoption of standards is a good enough reason to explore. The results will speak for themselves in rewards that will recoup the time investment exponentially.

The adoption of standardized solutions is not limited in scope to databases, but is applicable to most areas of any business and results in the prospect of other beneficial practices like code reuse, report formatting, naming conventions, and a myriad of virtually limitless other topics and areas. One of Vernon's first targets of standardization was reporting for their existing product, which focused on 30 customers that received nightly financial reports. Each customer had a slightly different report format where some wanted fields in a different order, others wanted some fields left out, and yet others wanted something completely different with pipe-limited choices, comma delimited, and whether they wanted field encapsulation or not. This meant that each time there was a table definition change that includes a field addition or removal, a database administrator was tasked with systematically modifying the jobs that produced the reports in each region for a customer from development through to production. Each time that code is modified adds another opportunity for human error to occur and not only was the formatting different for many of them, but the entire process for producing these reports was different as well. It was a jumble of shell scripts, stored procedures, and various other amalgamations that were thrown together to solve each customer's reporting solution, and each one different than the next.

The maintenance and support of these types of deployments are not sustainable unless one does not want their organization to spend time on work that is more beneficial to its continued business and survival. The first step is the identification of a potential candidate for standardization, the adoption of a standard, putting it into practice, and then the arduous task of maintaining it. The last two of these steps are the most difficult tasks when it comes to trying to adopt any level of standardization, but maintaining a standard is by far the most difficult in that it means sticking to it. In many cases this also means trying to make sure others stick to the standard practices, ultimately in some cases enforcing it, which in some cases makes one evil incarnate to those who would rather continue with the way things have always been done in the past. Change is too often not welcomed and standardizing practices where none have ever been before is a huge, but beneficial change that many fail to see the face value of.

Making use of the database migration as a driver, or catalyst, for change helped to alleviate the pressure and lackluster responses that result from making many improvements, including adding additional standardization and process improvement. For the team at FWP this meant getting out from under a closed proprietary DBMS as well as leveraging that change to help the organization evolve to the next level. There were many more areas for standardization besides the example of reporting that Vernon targeted that made a lasting impression on day to day operations. If one is considering evolving their business to a new platform that is in and of itself considered a disruptive change, they really should consider using that as a vehicle to improve the foundation of their business and its offerings. There really is no better time, and using it to provide an excuse for the often resisted rational of change is a strategy not to be overlooked.

Process Improvement

The analysis of day to day functions and how one's team spends their time is essential to taking a proactive approach in any industry, process, or task. Analyzing and creating an ordered target list by importance based on impact should be the first order when taking over anything from a managerial aspect if the intent is to improve and produce quality quantitative results. To be an effective leader and provide the highest level of operational consistency demands it, otherwise one is just coasting and continuing the business as usual standard, which is how businesses get left in the lurch in the technology sector every day. Constant evolution and improvement are not only expected but demanded, and anything else is just going through the motions.

Many managers, executives, and even business owners fall into the rut of business as usual. There is also the unfortunate effect where trying to improve business processes and operations can result in a target on one's back, as it is ingrained in human nature that change is a bad thing and to resist it comes all too naturally. This attitude is not one meant for the technology sector, because technology itself is changing on a daily basis as computers become more powerful and resources that just a few years ago were constrained are becoming almost limitless with advancements in memory, processing power, and storage capabilities. To not improve on processes and operations is the antithesis of the industry one is trying to be successful in, so a level of agility is required. To move towards Agile Methodologies is to move towards success, and to encompass these methodologies is to improve processes by the analysis and study of workflow.

Agile Methodologies and DevOps are two buzzwords that seem to get a lot of attention. Like most buzzwords they get abused by many in order to seem like they are on top of technology and adopting the latest and greatest, yet so few truly understand them. Agile and DevOps methodologies, just as with the term Open Source, have been practiced, been around, and implemented for many years without nearly the fanfare or the systemic vocal authority with lack of true understanding that they have gotten in more recent times. To be agile in the technology industry is to be open to and ready to adapt to change quickly. It is not just a software term, but a term that can be used to encompass all business practices targeting the areas of workflow and process improvement. Some database administrators may cringe at the thought of Agile Methodologies being applied to the database realm, but it does actually fit when encompassing the core of all that is Agile.

Work as well as workflow are much different for an applications developer or architect than they are for a database administrator, but that does not mean that one cannot implement Agile Methodologies from one standpoint and not the other. It just means that the methods implemented for one discipline may not, and in several cases are not, applicable to the other. During database application development an architect or developer may be working with requirements and changes that are changing rapidly, and thus the Agile Methods applied to their work is targeted appropriately. The database administrator on the other hand is generally handed a set of objects and/or object changes as part of the development team's work. These changes are then reviewed, feedback provided, and then implemented. The database administrator is then done and that is it until any other modifications or changes are requested, at which time the database team member is then reengaged by the development team. These two disciplines are very different, so as one can easily see their workflows and processes are different. One can easily grasp that this means that methodologies employed by one team are not going to necessarily work very well with the other; however, both can still be agile.

It does not make sense to have database team members sit through daily, sometimes twice-daily, stand-ups that development teams use in many interpretations or incarnations of Agile development methods. This is counterintuitive and accounts for time not well spent due to the nature of a database team and its role. For their part in the development process, once the database administrator has completed the targeted changes his/her job is done as far as release work. The database team's time is then spent on the other aspects of their jobs that are extremely important and take precedence in regard to supporting, maintaining, monitoring, and performance evaluations on both test and production environments. This is true especially at a smaller company where there the luxury of having database administrators teamed up in subdisciplines handling specialized and targeted areas does not exist.

In fact, Agile Methodologies can be applied to virtually any discipline or type of work in existence. The key word here is *work*. The study of work and workflow is the summation of implementing the Agile Methodology across multiple disciplines, with the desired effect being streamlining work in order that it flows continuously, even with occasional changes and hiccups, by alleviating wasted time and bottlenecks. This gets polluted and occasionally lost with the application across development teams; however, in its purest form it can be applied in any areas where work and workflow are involved.

DevOps is a more recent incarnation of Agile-related nomenclature that encompasses its methodologies across multiple teams in order to streamline work and its corresponding flow between teams. This has also been fraught with confusion and interpreted definitions, and in some cases used as a form of kingdom building in order to reign authority where it previously did not, and in most cases should not, exist. Even outside the financial sector where separation of duties is dictated by compliance and data security practices, there is a reason why disciplines exist across teams specialized in their area of expertise like Systems, Networking, Development, and of course Database teams. When one team, for example Development, decides that DevOps is the name of the game; convinces executive management of its warrants; and attempts a hostile takeover of other teams' duties, levels of access, or permissions; and insists on these things as requirements to do their job, it is not truly about DevOps or becoming Agile. This is not Agile and it most certainly is not DevOps, so buyer beware. DevOps in its truest nature is about applying analysis and strategies to interdepartmental work and its flow in order to improve it for expediting deliverables and implementations.

As previously discussed, the work and workflow for a database team is not like that of a development team, thus the same strategies implemented for them will turn out to be counterproductive. The new processes and requirements that Vernon had begun outlining as soon as he took over management of the database team were at their very core wrapped in the concepts of DevOps and becoming an Agile team without anyone ever knowing or realizing it. Taking advantage of the database migration was essential to successfully moving his team, their operations, and the services they provide into becoming a fully functional team operating on a level that had never been seen by the organization prior. This worked for them and it absolutely works in the real world.

The in-depth discussion of these methodologies is absolutely relative to the topic of migrating to the MariaDB solution in that these were used throughout the database migration. The migration served to further Vernon's goal to move the database team further away from a reactive approach, in effect aligning the team to embrace change as a much needed and required driver. The adoption and implementation of standards and then tactical improvement of processes served to move Vernon's team towards becoming a fully functional unit that provided quick response and service turn around. With the adoption of standards followed by improving processes, there was only one more aspect of fully bringing the team around and that was improved automation.

Automation

The final part, the best part, is the automation of solutions where applicable in order to provide Agile-like response and service from the database side of software development. To perform similar repetitive processes repeatedly, preferably without failure, is the auspicious endeavor behind the creation of machines by humankind. It also helps to move the database administrator discipline in the direction of being more intrinsic to Agile and DevOps principles. Looking at the bigger picture, successful automation is not possible without the act of standardization and the implementation of process improvement, and all three topics are included in the order provided specifically as a roadmap to be followed.

Computers are not unlike other machines that have been invented to serve in various roles of production of goods and services in that they are meant to perform repetitive work. The mantra here is that if one has to do the same process more than once, that process is viable for automation. First that process must be standardized, improved, and refined to the point that it makes automation possible. The automation of processes and procedures is in and of itself the improvement of work and the flow of work while taking the possibility of human error out of the equation, thus one can easily derive that automation itself is a big player in the Agile and DevOps game. These topics are precisely how one takes a database team into the arena.

Taking a hard look at the work and workflow of a team of database administrators, it has been established that neither fit the same mold as those of a development team, thus the approach must be different. The path that Vernon laid out was successful in its implementation of these principles and provides one the route to get there by following the same simple three-step process for virtually any team. First identify the process or problem and then run it through the following three steps:

1.   Standardize the solution.

2.   Refine and improve the process.

3.   Once the process is refined to the point of being easily repeatable, automate it.

Vernon applied this same methodology to reporting by first adopting a standardized format that each customer could expect and could count on getting without question. For their team it was as simple as adopting the IETF (Internet Engineering Task Force) RFC-4180 standard for CSV (Comma Separated Values) using comma separated and double quotes encapsulated fields, new line for each record, and no field reordering or other customized requests. This meant that all reporting would be the same across the board without question. The next step was to develop a process for taking data out of the database and then write to a report file formatted with this new standard. This process then went through several stages of refinement and improvements in order to be used across every FWP customer's platform. This culminated in one program that could be automated and used to run the same standardized reports for every different customer by being passed a parameter file specific to each targeted customer. This was something that had never been accomplished before, and it brought to fruition much of what Vernon had been trying to do both in person and behind the scenes in order to bring about beneficial engineered change with his team.

Note   The full RFC-4180 specification can be found here: `https://tools.ietf.org/html/rfc4180`.

The example here that was applied to reporting encompasses the principles as discussed by first standardizing a product or process and then refining that process to the point that it is a robust solution improving both workflow and the customer experience. This is exactly what Agile and DevOps are meant to be by definition, in that it improved the database team's workflow and work output exponentially. They were no longer spending long hours trying to maintain, troubleshoot, and support a mismatched hodgepodge set of solutions that were different for every customer, and it helped ferret out some of the tribal knowledge mentality that had become engrained at FWP. This meant more time could be spent on other tasks and bottlenecks that would further improve the performance and response of the database team, tasks that previously would get pushed aside due to time sinks such as reporting. This all served to facilitate making the team function in a much more Agile fashion approaching true DevOps principles.

CHAPTER 7

Defining a Roadmap for Success

Taking on such a monumental technology task as migrating to a different DBMS solution involves equally monumental risks, and the only way to mitigate those risks is through proper analysis, planning, testing, and implementation. Not to minimize other areas of technology, but migrating database solutions carries an extraordinary risk in comparison.

At the top of the risk chain is the data itself, and minimizing any threat by mistake or otherwise to that data is priority number one. In the effort to maintain the data in its integrity, and entirety, there are no shortcuts that can be taken. Following standard, everyday database administration policies fits this task and there is no replacement for taking the extra time to perform backup procedures and validating them prior to any big change, especially migrating to a new DBMS. If one's business relies on data and that data is stored in a DBMS to be migrated, having a clearly analyzed and defined roadmap that matches your requirements and deployment is the only way to get there successfully.

The following is a look at the roadmap that was defined by Vernon and the team at Financial Widgets Plus (FWP) in order to migrate from their existing Oracle RAC deployment to the MariaDB solution. Their roadmap was a phased approach using the principles of KISS that started with a simple replication setup and eventually migrated that to a full MariaDB Galera Cluster deployment.

© William Wood 2019
W. Wood, *Migrating to MariaDB*, https://doi.org/10.1007/978-1-4842-3997-1_7

Database Evaluation

One's current database solution should be firmly understood as part of developing a roadmap, as well as to validate that the solution is accurate. The team at FWP completed multiple deep dives into their current solution in order to match up any possible replacements. The creation of visual representations of the database topology as well as solutions that were driven from them helped to relay this information to those with less technical skills or with skills in other technical areas. This helped to drive down key requirements in a new database solution to the bare minimum.

The evaluation and prioritizing of the most important requirements are tantamount in that this allowed for reducing potential solutions quickly while saving time for the next evaluation. For Vernon's team, many possible solutions were quickly dismissed due to identifying these requirements with a thorough analysis:

- Encryption for data at rest and data in transit

- Cost effectiveness

- Licensing simplicity

- Security

- Ease of porting existing code

Requirements creation saved their team a lot of time and helped them to quickly identify MariaDB as a potential candidate quickly and easily. Someone else might have differing requirements, possibly less stringent or more; however, the first part of the roadmap is defining those requirements. This will save one's organization time, money, and resources.

Evaluating MariaDB involved not only database technology but also the application side. The successful deployment to a new DBMS is going to be a failure if the application that it is driving does not function and the preexisting functionality, both application side and database side, does not work. This is where one must be extremely fastidious in investigating functionality and in making sure that it migrates along with everything else.

Migrating low-level database objects from one database technology to another is tedious work. Mapping datatypes from one solution to the other is generally the first line of order that then carries through with the deployment of table definitions. Using the example of the folks at FWP, the first line of order was creating a script that included MariaDB SQL for table creation, defining primary keys, and indexes. The datatype mapping from Oracle datatypes to MariaDB datatypes was then completed by parsing out one datatype for its replacement. There are tools that will do this for you; however, after a couple of tests Vernon concluded that it was faster and easier to just dump the table creation statements from Oracle, parse them into MariaDB table creation syntax, and then parse in the corrected datatypes.

Once the table objects were all created in MariaDB, the next step was to migrate the lower level database programming code, which involved triggers, stored procedures, and functions. Since MariaDB supports PL/SQL, all of the database side programming logic was moved with a few minor changes due to Oracle built-ins that of course do not exist in MariaDB. Since the first phase of migrating the database was getting the table definitions migrated, this made it very easy to test the lower level database programming logic. Vernon and the team actually found flawed logic that existed in Oracle for a very long time that they were able to fix on the MariaDB side. When dealing with any kind of legacy code or database logic, one must expect to run into these little hidden gems and account for them in the overall project timeline.

Once the database side of the migration was complete, the database team then began focusing on the database administration portions of the solution. At this point in time in the project for FWP, a backup solution that worked with the data encryption functionality in MariaDB did not exist. They initially started with using mysqldump as a backup and then those database dumps would be archived, zipped, and encrypted. The team at MariaDB has now ported xtrabackup, which works with MariaDB data encryption, can do incremental backups, and also encrypt the resultant backup as well.

The next step in the migration was to get an application server deployed with the Standardized Financial Widgets code and the new connection daemons to evaluate the new solution. This is also a point where legacy code can very well cause an abrupt halt; however, for their team everything appeared to function with no major hurdles or issues. It was time to decide on a first customer to migrate to the new solution with MariaDB driving the backend.

Evaluating First Steps

The first steps that fit a small organization like FWP were defined to fit their available resources and limits therein. The approach was on the conservative side and all work was completed in a phased approach in order to limit the resources spent. A larger firm with more staff and resources could very well modify this approach, deciding on either replication or clustering for their solution of choice.

Any organization that is contemplating a migration from Oracle to MariaDB would find the first steps as defined by Vernon and his team applicable. That was a list of just ten steps to achieve a migration onto the MariaDB platform:

1. Fully evaluate the candidate solution

    a. Does it fit the most important requirements?

2. Deploy a sandbox environment

3. Test thoroughly with similar objects that are leveraged by the application

4. Refine the solution, as with FWP

    a. Standalone

    b. Replication

    c. Clustering

    d. Backups

    e. Automation

5. Deploy development environment for initial testing

6. Evaluate legacy issues for improvement

7. Deploy Testing and QA environment

8. Thoroughly test application code with all possible QA analysis including regression testing

9. Continue rollout with User Acceptance Testing environment

10. Full production go-live

FWP looked at several potential solutions that never made it past step number one, so the existence of these defined steps was tantamount to saving them considerable time and resources. Having a roadmap is helpful no matter what the sizing or resource constraints may be for any organization. This strategy is not limited to database changes either; it can be leveraged for virtually any type of change and helps identify a roadmap to fruition of change.

Path of Least Resistance

No roadmap would be complete without bringing up KISS once again in the strategy of choosing a path of least resistance to arrive at the desired outcome. This may mean choosing a customer that leverages a simpler, possibly newer, or standardized version of one's software offering, like what Vernon and the rest of the team at FWP chose to do. Choosing a customer to go first meant working any bugs or complications out in a simple environment as compared with starting with the most complex application out of the box.

Being resource minded and with differing customers that ranged from simple software as a service with service calls, to customers with full out functionality for the financial industry to process information, the team needed to pick a first customer to migrate. The KISS methodology was again put into action by choosing the easiest customer with the least functionality to migrate to the new database solution. For the team at FWP, this meant that they would be doing a full evaluation of the MariaDB solution in many ways.

The one customer that came to mind was not only their customer of least resistance from a service and code side point of view, but they were also one of their highest transactional customers. Out of all of the customers they had, this customer did by far the highest amount of transactions per day in their peak season. For Vernon and the database team, this meant not only would they be testing out the new database backend on the first customer from a migration standpoint, but also from a performance perspective. This meant projecting transaction statistics and getting the new database solution configured to meet the expected load and processing capabilities out of the starting gate.

Following a path of least resistance works hand in hand with the KISS principle as one is building on their solution and layering in the complexity over time. This is a principle gleamed from the definition of DevOps in that it lessened a potential bottleneck of spending huge resources on the application code migration by starting with a customer's deployment that had been scoped as one of the easiest to migrate with the lowest level of complexity. This worked, and it worked well because so much was gleamed from migrating the first customer that customers with much more complex deployments turned out to be easier.

Success

It seems whimsical that such a huge endeavor involved with migrating from Oracle RAC to an Open Source Database could be described as an exercise in making a change in ten steps, but in synopsis, those were the steps followed as outlined. It has been done so successfully with MariaDB, first in the real world by the author and second by the fictional Vernon and the rest of the team at FWP.

It was all the work between the lines in those ten steps to success that made it happen, with all of the analysis work, deep dives into database code, application code functionality, and mapping solutions from one DBMS to the next. This migration took many hours of resources and time that went on behind the scenes, especially on the database team with all of the analysis and design work, in order for it to have been successful. The MariaDB solution is a proven replacement for the Oracle database with its built-in encryption for secure applications.

CHAPTER 8

Making the Data Move

The next phase in migrating to MariaDB (from Oracle in particular) is making the data move from one DBMS to another successfully, and this was the part of the migration that was very important for Financial Widgets Plus (FWP) to get right for the existing customers and their corresponding production data. All new customers coming into the program would go straight to the new database solution; however, they needed to get an existing customer out there and running as a proof of concept.

There are many vendor products that are written to specifically migrate data between different database solutions and can even do dual write as part of that functionality. This would make the data much easier to migrate and have up to date. There are a few caveats with these solutions such as high cost, and getting to a point in time can be time consuming in that if anything fails during the process one may be stuck starting back over. Vernon and the team researched many solutions and their corresponding price tags; however, what they needed for doing this was already in house with their connection state solutions that already existed. They could have a daemon running for an Oracle connection and a separate disjoint daemon running for the MariaDB solution with no interruption to ongoing transactions due to time, performance, or load on the MariaDB side. This would be a great goal to shoot for in getting FWP on the road to becoming database agnostic.

The scenario that comes to mind would be related to retention scenarios, thereby maintaining the legacy database as the primary database for read and writes while sending all writes to the new database

© William Wood 2019
W. Wood, *Migrating to MariaDB*, https://doi.org/10.1007/978-1-4842-3997-1_8

at the same time. This methodology would allow the new database to catch up to the legacy database and FWP to pick a hard cutover date to coincide with the purging constraints. If the purging constraints are 90 days, then dual writing would be performed for 90 days, and then all transaction reading and writing operations would migrate from the legacy database to the new database.

With dual write having great potential for large databases with volumes of data, once Vernon's team stepped up to working on the data migrations it was found that most customers could be moved within an acceptable window. The following sections will describe in fairly concise detail how they went about performing these migrations successfully and how they arrived at that point.

First Steps

The initial phase of data migration involved multiple teams getting together and discussing the possibilities. It was during these discussions that the team of Software Architects stepped up and offered to move the data over programmatically. This was a great idea because their help would be needed in order to facilitate dual writes in the not so distant future, so their involvement was readily accepted.

With the architect team taking over the task of moving the data from Oracle to MariaDB, it left Vernon's team the time to do more work on the actual implementation and deployment side of the solution. This appeared to be a win-win solution, at least initially. The problems started to crop up as time progressed and required time from the database team.

There were initially two problems with the first attempted solution in that the processes that maintain the connection state could not handle extremely large tables or large object (LOB) data. The memory capabilities of these daemons prohibited copying large data objects as well as tables with a large column count successfully, so this meant some changes were going to be required. The database team would write the code to dump the LOB data types and load them into the database while the architect team would modify the code to handle a subset of columns for a large table incrementally.

During the development phase of the database move for large objects, Vernon decided to write his code to handle all possible tables and pertinent data types. This turned out to be a good move and a great learning experience that reinforced that going by instinct can pay off in dividends.

Letting DBAs be DBAs

It is not easily discernable why it exists this way, but experience has dictated that many folks know how to perform and want to do the work that would normally fall under a database administrator no matter what the field. This does not mean to say that they are not capable; rather, it infers that database administrators deal with these things on a day to day basis and generally have a much deeper knowledge on database topics. In some cases this help may actually be warranted but in others it just adds an additional dynamic, making the database administrator's job harder. Looking at it from Vernon's perspective at FWP, dealing with this was one of the biggest struggles in his career and directly relative to completing a huge migration like this successfully.

For any management level and cross-departmental folks intending to get some insight from this work, the biggest concept to grasp onto here is to let your DBAs be DBAs. In a positive environment, everyone will want to chip in and help; this is a good thing. In a competitive environment, everyone will want to chip in for the sake of downplaying another team or another person's involvement, especially with a project with the scope of migrating to a new database solution as the eyes on a project this monumental are significant. If you have a competent database staff for resources, then let them do their job.

One of the hurdles that Vernon saw on a day to day basis was that even though the services they provided were web-based database-driven technologies, seldom were the DBAs ever involved other than receiving a work order to perform database changes. This mentality had resulted in some very bad designs making their way to implementation with an attitude that if you asked questions, made observations, or came up with a better solution that it was too late to change anything because the customer wanted it in production right away. If anyone fought this mentality or said anything about it, they were suddenly difficult to work with, combative, and the list goes on. This was not a good collaborative environment.

Choosing his battles and limited acquiescence had become a tool kit that Vernon began to rely on when dealing with these hurdles. Provide enough rope for someone to hang themselves and have a solution ready to go when it happened. This is precisely the playbook he used for the data migration portion of the project. If the architects succeeded then that would be great and save some DBA time; however, if it failed he wanted to have a solution ready to go and that is exactly what happened with one of the first migrations. The development process for the migration in a production environment failed and failed miserably, but the database portion with the large data objects worked fine. This provided the vehicle for him to approach this in a manner to get the other teams to allow his team to be DBAs and do the work of a DBA by overseeing and migrating the existing data.

The migration of the existing data is the next step that will be covered: first, by building a knowledge tool kit with the functionality and description of the tools used in the data migration process. The tool kit that will be built here will then provide the solid foundation for making the data move from Oracle to MariaDB by relying on resources and functionality that already exist, with no additional costs.

Tool Building

A huge part of one's experience over many years in the technology sector is learning many different tools and utilities to make their work easier. The Oracle database solution has some built-in packages and tools that come in handy, not just for day to day operations, but that can be very useful in migrating off of the DBMS itself. After looking at many different options, these are what Vernon decided to leverage in order to facilitate the data migration from Oracle to MariaDB. There is some irony in the fact that one can use Oracle's own tools in order to be free of their product.

Oracle has many built-in packages that can be taken advantage of from a database programming level using PL/SQL, and one of those is the UTL_FILE package that allows queried data to be written to the file system into flat files with formatting. This package is very useful for any kind of reporting that requires special formatting when pulling data out of an Oracle database. There are many different ways that could be used to pull data out of one database and import it to another; there are several vendors that offer database management studios that can not only migrate the data but also keep it in sync. The team at FWP leveraged this package to pull data from Oracle to MariaDB dumped into insert statements that conformed to SQL 99 that could then be batch loaded into the new database solution.

There are many different parameters and function calls in the UTL_FILE package; however, for this exercise we are concerned with what is required to make the data move from one database to another. It is always advisable to learn more about any type of utility or package when using it in order to grasp a firm understanding of what a particular tool, or set of tools, is capable of. However, for this the requirement is very simple in that one needs to know how to open a file for writing, write to the file, and then close it once it is complete. The following functions are to be levied:

- FOPEN
  - Opens and creates a file handle
- FCLOSE
  - Closes the file handle
- FFLUSH
  - Flushes any string remnants in the buffer to the file handle
- PUT
  - Writes a string to file handle
- PUT_LINE
  - Writes line to file handle and appends OS specific line terminator
- PUT_RAW
  - Writes raw data o file handle in binary form; in this exercise it is necessary for writing LOB data types such as BLOB and CLOB.

FOPEN

The FOPEN procedure is used to open a file handle to a specified file name and location as passed from the calling program, and is dependent on the mode it is opened in. See Listing 8-1 for the usage statement. The parameters that are passed to FOPEN are very important in relation to the

requirements and have been listed here along with a description of the
expected parameters when calling the function:

- location: string with the full directory path where file is
  to be created

- filename: string designating the name of the file to be
  created

- open_mode: the mode in which the file should be
  opened

  - r - read

  - w - write

  - a - append

  - rb - read in byte mode

  - wb - write in byte mode

  - ab - append in byte mode

- max_linesize: is an integer designating the max number
  of characters to be written in a line

  - minimum = 1

  - maxmimum = 32767

  - default = 1024

Listing 8-1. FOPEN

```
UTL_FILE.FOPEN (location     IN VARCHAR2,
 filename      IN VARCHAR2,
 open_mode     IN VARCHAR2,
 max_linesize IN BINARY_INTEGER DEFAULT 1024)
 RETURN FILE_TYPE;
```

The FOPEN procedure when called will return a file handle. This can be stored in a named variable for easy access and calling throughout a PL/SQL program.

FCLOSE

The FCLOSE procedure closes the file handle as created with the FOPEN procedure. See Listing 8-2 for the usage statement. Proper programming etiquette would be to always make sure that if you open a file, or file handle, that it should be closed within the code as well. If the file is not closed, it will potentially remain locked and inaccessible.

Listing 8-2. FCLOSE

```
UTL_FILE.FCLOSE (file_handle IN OUT FILE_TYPE);
```

FFLUSH

The FFLUSH function writes any pending string data in the buffer to the file handle. See Listing 8-3 for the usage statement.

Listing 8-3. FFLUSH

```
UTL_FILE.FFLUSH (file_handle IN FILE_TYPE);
```

PUT

The PUT procedure places a text string from the buffer to the open file handle without any new line formatting characters. See Listing 8-4 for the usage statement. The buffer is written as is.

The parameter list for PUT consists of just two parameters:

- file_handle: name of the file handle being passed
- buffer: buffer size
  - default = 1024
  - maximum = 32767

Listing 8-4. PUT

```
UTL_FILE.PUT (file_handle IN FILE_TYPE,
 buffer IN VARCHAR2);
```

PUT_LINE

The PUT_LINE procedure is almost identical to the PUT procedure except it appends the operating system pertinent line termination string to the end of the passed string and can be set with a boolean value for automatic buffer flushing. Please see Listing 8-5 for the usage statement.

The parameter list for the PUT_LINE procedure consists of the following:

- file_handle: name of the file handle being passed
- buffer: buffer size
  - default = 1024
  - maximum = 32767
- autoflush: boolean value for automatic buffer flush after the write operation is complete

Listing 8-5. PUT_LINE

```
UTL_FILE.PUT_LINE (file_handle IN FILE_TYPE,
 buffer IN VARCHAR2,
 autoflush IN BOOLEAN DEFAULT FALSE);
```

Note   The maximum buffer size for both PUT and PUT_LINE is 32767; however, take special note that the buffer must be flushed prior to any consecutive calls to either procedure.

Review of the PUT and PUT_LINE procedures will make it readily apparent under which circumstances one should use either. If writing a full line at once, then PUT_LINE is easier; however, logic dictates that the PUT procedure can be used as well with a follow up PUT placing a new line character. This results in superfluous code that could be better written by using the correct tool for the desired results.

PUT_RAW

The PUT_RAW procedure within the UTL_FILE package is used for writing raw data to a file handle, such as large objects that must be written in binary mode. See Listing 8-6 for the usage statement. One caveat that will be seen later when these topics are all put together is that in many instances the same tables that contain raw data will also contain descriptive constraint fields with regular data types that must be pulled too. The simple workaround for this is:

1.   Close the file handle with FCLOSE.

2.   Recreate the same file handle with FOPEN in append byte mode(ab).

3.   Write the binary data.

4.   Close the file handle in binary mode with FCLOSE.

5.   Recreate the file handle with FOPEN in append mode(a).

The parameter list for the PUT_LINE procedure consists of the following:

- file_handle: name of the file handle being passed

- buffer: buffer size

  - default = 1024

  - maximum = 32767

- autoflush: boolean value for automatic buffer flush after the write operation is complete

Listing 8-6. PUT_RAW

```
UTL_FILE.PUT_RAW (file_handle IN FILE_TYPE,
 buffer IN VARCHAR2,
 autoflush IN BOOLEAN DEFAULT FALSE);
```

The use of PUT_RAW procedures is the last procedure that is part of the data migration solution; however, as with all things one is encouraged to increase their knowledge base by becoming familiar with more of the functionality built into the UTL_FILE package.

These procedures give one the building blocks in regard to using Oracle's UTL_FILE package in order to create output at the file system level, and can be used for everything from reporting to dumping properly formatted insert statements for batch loading for data migrations. There are other ways to do this and one should explore multiple avenues in order to arrive at the best case scenario that augments their specific setups and deployments.

Dynamic SQL

Dynamic SQL is a very powerful tool that makes it possible to generate SQL on the fly when working across databases where tables are not identical, and it also helps to alleviate a lot of hard coded queries, thus lowering the maintenance and support of one's code. When working across multiple customer databases there might be similarly named tables that do not share the exact same fields, which could make it a nightmare to support when migrating a large number of customer databases as one would need to update their code for each table. The Oracle DBMS has another great package that we can exploit here called DBMS_SQL.

The DBMS_SQL package is another Oracle package that provides a great vehicle for database programming (for which only the surface will be scratched) in order to satisfy the requirements in the migration of data that may have similar but disjoint definitions across multiple databases. A database generally consists of many tables, which consist of many columns of varying data types, and to try to write reusable, sustainable, and manageable code would be next to impossible without the ability to generate code specific to all these variable table definitions.

With such a wide array of variance across tables in regard to data types, field lengths, and field names there is only a small bit of information one would need to be able to dynamically select information about a specific table on the fly. Different data types will need to be handled with respect to their data type, and there are many system views that can be used to get this information. One such view is the all_tab_columns view that contains information specific to each column in a table. There are two pieces of information that one needs to know in order to perform processing of the table data:

- Number of columns in the target table

- Name of the columns of the target table

The number of columns is needed to loop through the all_tab_cols view in order to obtain information specific to each column; however, we can get both values from the same view. In order to find the number of columns in a table, a simple select is used with the count function; an example is provided in Listing 8-7. One can then use the results of this in order to loop through each of the columns in the table to obtain information specific to each column, as seen in Listing 8-8. These two queries provide the basis for using dynamic SQL to not just be able to dump one table's data, but by using this information the same can be run on each table by passing a table or potentially a list of tables.

Listing 8-7. Obtaining the Number of Columns in a Table

```
select count(*) from all_tab_columns where owner = 'target_
schema' and table_name = 'target_table';
```

Note   Use the oracle describe command to view the definition of any table or view:
mysql> describe table_name;

Listing 8-8. Obtaining a List of Column Names for a Table

```
select column_name from all_tab_columns where owner =
'target_schema' and table_name='table_name';
```

These two queries can now be used as the basis for generating table-specific information on the fly. Assuming that one has a PL/SQL procedure that is called with two variables that contain the owner (schema name) and the table name as in_owner and in_table, respectively, this provides the capability to grab this information to any set of owners and tables that the user has access to. This information can then be stored into variables for further processing.

A sample stored procedure is provided in Listing 8-9 that first queries the number of columns in the specific table and then uses a cursor in order to loop through the view to obtain the column name for each column of the target table. Notice the use of bind variables and the DBMS_SQL package in this example.

Listing 8-9. Table Information Procedure

```
create or replace procedure table_info(in_table varchar2,in_
owner varchar2)
is
v_row_num              NUMBER;
v_nothing              NUMBER;
v_count                NUMBER;
v_colid                NUMBER;
v_colname              VARCHAR2(32);
sqlStr_hdr             VARCHAR2(4096);
hdr_rslts              VARCHAR2(4096);
hdr_cols               VARCHAR2(4096);
begin
execute immediate ('select count(*) from  all_tab_columns
where owner = :1 and table_name = :2') into v_row_num using
in_owner,in_table;
sqlStr_hdr:='select column_name from all_tab_columns where
owner = :1 and table_name = :2 order by column_id';
v_colid := dbms_sql.open_cursor;
DBMS_SQL.PARSE(v_colid,sqlStr_hdr,dbms_sql.native);
DBMS_SQL.BIND_VARIABLE(v_colid, ':1', in_owner);
DBMS_SQL.BIND_VARIABLE(v_colid, ':2', in_table);
DBMS_SQL.DEFINE_COLUMN(v_colid,1,v_colname,1024);
v_nothing := DBMS_SQL.EXECUTE(v_colid);
v_count := 0;
WHILE DBMS_SQL.FETCH_ROWS(v_colid) > 0 LOOP
 DBMS_SQL.COLUMN_VALUE(v_colid, 1, v_colname);
 hdr_cols := hdr_cols||v_colname;
 hdr_rslts := hdr_rslts||v_colname;
 v_count := v_count + 1;
```

```
 if (v_count < v_row_num) then
   hdr_cols := hdr_cols||',';
   hdr_rslts := hdr_rslts||',';
 end if;
END LOOP;
DBMS_SQL.CLOSE_CURSOR(v_colid);
dbms_output.put_line(hdr_cols);
dbms_output.put_line(hdr_rslts);
END table_info;
/
```

This stored procedure can be created on any Oracle database, and when called properly with server output enabled will provide the output of two strings created as a comma separated list containing the names of each column in the table. See Listing 8-10 as an example of running the stored procedure at the command line.

Listing 8-10. Execute Stored Procedure

```
SQL> set serveroutput on;
SQL> exec table_info('table_name','table_owner');
     column1,column2,column3,column4
     column1,column2,column3,column4

     PL/SQL procedure succesfully completed.

SQL>
```

This is a really good starting point on the way to being able to dump migration data into properly formatted insert statements; however, there is still one other thing that is missing. With data type mapping exercises it is know that Oracle and MariaDB store dates and timestamps differently, not to mention we also have to deal with LOB data types, so these data types will need to be formatted properly for insert into the new database.

This means in order to process this data programmatically, the data type of each column must be known at or before run time. Before run time would mean lots of coding, so let's look at how it can be done dynamically at run time by pulling information regarding the data types used in the specific Oracle database version and their type codes while comparing it with those used by the database being migrated.

Pulling out some simple SQL in SQLPLUS against the same view that has been used for our other requirements, it is quite simple to obtain a list of the data types used by a specific database. The sample query and results in Listing 8-11 provide exactly what is needed with one of Financial Widget Plus's customers. One could spend the time coding for every possible data type; however, this saves some considerable development time by sticking to the requirements to get the job done.

Listing 8-11. Quering Data Types in Use by a Customer Database

```
SQL> select distinct data_type from all_tab_columns where
owner='FWP_CUST1';
DATA_TYPE
--------------------------------------------------------
TIMESTAMP(6)
NUMBER
CLOB
CHAR
DATE
VARCHAR2
BLOB

7 rows selected.

SQL>
```

FWP customer database FWP_CUST1 is using only seven data types throughout their entire database. Knowing this information makes the conversion much easier and short circuits the time involved in having to provide the logic flow for only the data types at play. There is still a piece of the puzzle missing in that when using DBMS_SQL package function desc_ tab the data type code. This information can be found on the Internet, Oracle documentation, and via the query in Listing 8-12 along with the results. For completeness, the database this was run on was Oracle 12.1.0.2.0. The most appropriate would be what comes directly out of your database version, so the use of the query is recommended.

Listing 8-12. Obtaining a List of Data Types and Type Codes Direct from Local Database

```
SQL> select text from all_source where owner = 'SYS' and name =
'DBMS_TYPES' and type='PACKAGE';
PACKAGE dbms_types AS
  TYPECODE_DATE            PLS_INTEGER :=  12;
  TYPECODE_NUMBER          PLS_INTEGER :=   2;
  TYPECODE_RAW             PLS_INTEGER :=  95;
  TYPECODE_CHAR            PLS_INTEGER :=  96;
  TYPECODE_VARCHAR2        PLS_INTEGER :=   9;
  TYPECODE_VARCHAR         PLS_INTEGER :=   1;
  TYPECODE_MLSLABEL        PLS_INTEGER := 105;
  TYPECODE_BLOB            PLS_INTEGER := 113;
  TYPECODE_BFILE           PLS_INTEGER := 114;
  TYPECODE_CLOB            PLS_INTEGER := 112;
  TYPECODE_CFILE           PLS_INTEGER := 115;
  TYPECODE_TIMESTAMP       PLS_INTEGER := 187;
  TYPECODE_TIMESTAMP_TZ    PLS_INTEGER := 188;
  TYPECODE_TIMESTAMP_LTZ   PLS_INTEGER := 232;
  TYPECODE_INTERVAL_YM     PLS_INTEGER := 189;
```

```
  TYPECODE_INTERVAL_DS      PLS_INTEGER := 190;
  TYPECODE_REF              PLS_INTEGER := 110;
  TYPECODE_OBJECT           PLS_INTEGER := 108;
  TYPECODE_VARRAY           PLS_INTEGER := 247;
/* COLLECTION TYPE */
  TYPECODE_TABLE            PLS_INTEGER := 248;
/* COLLECTION TYPE */
  TYPECODE_NAMEDCOLLECTION PLS_INTEGER := 122;
  TYPECODE_OPAQUE           PLS_INTEGER := 58;
/* OPAQUE TYPE */
/* NOTE: These typecodes are for use in AnyData api only and
are short forms for the corresponding char typecodes with a
charset form of SQLCS_NCHAR.*/
  TYPECODE_NCHAR            PLS_INTEGER := 286;
  TYPECODE_NVARCHAR2        PLS_INTEGER := 287;
  TYPECODE_NCLOB            PLS_INTEGER := 288;
/* Typecodes for Binary Float, Binary Double and Urowid. */
  TYPECODE_BFLOAT           PLS_INTEGER := 100;
  TYPECODE_BDOUBLE          PLS_INTEGER := 101;
  TYPECODE_UROWID           PLS_INTEGER := 104;
  SUCCESS                   PLS_INTEGER := 0;
  NO_DATA                   PLS_INTEGER := 100;
/* Exceptions */
  invalid_parameters EXCEPTION;
  PRAGMA EXCEPTION_INIT(invalid_parameters, -22369);
  incorrect_usage EXCEPTION;
  PRAGMA EXCEPTION_INIT(incorrect_usage, -22370);
  type_mismatch EXCEPTION;
  PRAGMA EXCEPTION_INIT(type_mismatch, -22626);
END dbms_types;
```

This last piece of the puzzle now provides everything needed to move forward with dynamically creating formatted insert statements that conform to SQL 99 and provide an avenue for data migration.

Handling LOB Data

The handling of LOB data types is not an easy task when it comes to the Oracle database. It is easy to get large data objects in, but getting them back out again can be a completely different matter. Pulling large objects back out of the database requires a bit more programming logic and work in order to do it consistently and successfully. This process gets compounded for the benefit of producing specifically formatted results such as insert statements, reports, and the like.

The first thing to draw one's attention is that magical number that we have already seen a significant amount of times in this chapter, 32767. That golden number is the max buffer size for many Oracle functions and procedures. If one's requirements entail pulling out a 4-GB file from database storage, it has to be done in increments that are less than or equal to this number. This buffer size requires close scrutiny and attention, as many built-in procedures have this same limitation that affects the amount of data that can be pulled out and processed at any one time. So if your large objects are stored in an encoded format, such as PDF documents in base64, the logic must allow for that. Also, as noted previously this buffer must be flushed for sequential use, otherwise the results will be incorrect resulting in data that is no longer valid or usable.

Note   When using a buffer size and adding escape characters, one must be aware that any formatting characters will change the size of the data in the bugger.

Using the utilities that have been discussed up to this point, one only needs to add a little program logic to loop through any type of LOB data and write it to a file that can then be easily migrated to the new database. In Vernon's case the only types of LOBs that had to be handled were BLOB and CLOB datatypes. Listing 8-13 provides a portion of code that includes an if statement to ascertain that the datatype is a CLOB. The logic then proceeds to close out the current file handle to then open it in append mode writing in binary to the file. The next steps are then to loop through the LOB datatype and write it in chunks to the migration file while escaping any special characters. One caveat of dumping LOB datatypes with the utl_file utility is that the file must be opened in binary mode. Dumping full tables that have many columns with differing datatypes requires first closing the file and then opening it back up in binary mode.

Listing 8-13. Looping Through CLOB Data and Writing to File

```
ELSIF (v_desctab(i).col_type = 112) THEN
   DBMS_SQL.COLUMN_VALUE(v_curid, i, v_clob_var);
   IF v_clob_var IS NOT NULL THEN
     utl_file.put(out_file,"");
     utl_file.fclose(out_file);
     out_file := utl_file.fopen(in_dir,v_file_name,'ab',32767);
     l_length := DBMS_LOB.getlength(v_clob_var);
     v_pdf_var := dbms_lob.substr(v_clob_var,4,1);
     while ( l_offset < l_length )
     Loop
       v_cvchar := dbms_lob.substr(v_clob_var,l_amt,l_offset);
       v_cvchar := replace(v_cvchar, '\',");
       v_cvchar := replace(v_cvchar,"", '\"');
       v_cvchar := replace(v_cvchar,'"', '\"');
       utl_file.put_raw(out_file,utl_raw.cast_to_raw(v_cvchar));
       l_offset := l_offset + l_amt;
     end loop;
```

```
    l_offset := 1;
    utl_file.fclose(out_file);
    out_file := UTL_FILE.fopen(in_dir,v_file_name,'a', 32767);
    utl_file.put(out_file,'"');
  ELSE
    utl_file.put(out_file,'NULL');
  END IF;
```

There are other ways to dump data from an Oracle database besides using PL/SQL. This does work, it works well, and unless one is working with extremely large datasets it is fast. Some performance improvements are certainly possible with Pro *C and potentially leveraging expensive utilities to do the same work; however, this adheres well to the KISS principle and it works. The formatting of the resulting database feed file can easily be modified to suit ones needs or application.

Listing 8-14. LOAD DATA INFILE Usage Statement

```
LOAD DATA [LOW_PRIORITY | CONCURRENT] [LOCAL] INFILE
'<file_name>'   [REPLACE | IGNORE]   INTO TABLE <table_
name>   [CHARACTER SET charset_name]   [{FIELDS |
COLUMNS}       [TERMINATED BY '<string>']       [[OPTIONALLY]
ENCLOSED BY '<escape_char>']      [ESCAPED BY
'<escape_char>']    ]   [LINES      [STARTING BY
'<string>']      [TERMINATED BY '<string>']    ]   [IGNORE
number LINES]   [(col_name_or_variable,...)]    [SET col_name
= expr,...]
```

Working with LOB data, in the form of characters or binary, is straightforward in a logic loop when the data is encoded. Luckily for the team at FWP, all LOB files stored as binary data were base64 encoded, so that is the example that will be covered. The problem with binary data that isn't encoded is not dumping it out of the Oracle database, but in the process of loading it into MariaDB. This is easily resolved by dumping these unencoded binary objects into files and using the LOAD DATA INFILE utility. See Listing 8-14 for the usage statement. The examples provided here only need a little modification to handle these types of loads if one runs across them in their own migration. Listing 8-15 provides an example on using the LOAD DATA utility. In this example we are loading a file into a test table that has fields that are comma terminated, enclosed by double quotes, and special characters that are escaped with and escape character. The final parameter passed for LINES TERMINATED BY is not mandatory; however, when dealing with large characters it can be easier to designate a string that signifies end of line for each record. This is not the only way to load data into MariaDB and in some cases a mixed approach might be required.

Listing 8-15. Using LOAD DATA INFILE Example

```
LOAD DATA INFILE '/<directory>/<path>/<file_name>' INTO test_
table_a FIELDS TERMINATED BY ',' ENCLOSED BY '"' ESCAPED BY
'<escape_char>' LINES TERMINATED BY '\n<record_end>\n';
```

Another approach to loading data would be to dump the data into properly formatted SQL insert statements. If one's application relies on the manipulation of data with triggers, the best manner in migrating data would be to use insert statements as the vehicle to move data for any tables that lie within that scope. This will save significant time as compared with going back after the data has moved and manipulating it; it also removes human error that can crop up during this process. Let the database programming do that work for you.

Sample Solution Code

The methods and utilities discussed here can be leveraged when migrating to, and from, any database solution that supports some method of loading bulk data as well as PL/SQL. Oracle's database solution has a magnanimous amount of functionality built into it, so well that it is perfectly viable to leverage that same functionality to migrate off their DBMS if required. It is a great solution, as is the cost; however, the following code is provided here as working examples.

The first example, provided in Listing 8-16, can be used to write properly formatted load files using SQL 99 formatted insert statements. This sample will create an insert statement load file that can be used with a wide variety of data types by ascertaining the data type it is working with. Each field is appended by creating an insert statement based on that record. This works great when lower level database programming logic exists based on row operations like an insert or update. A solution where this might come in to play would be with metrics-based reporting where a reporting table, or tables, exist to provide statistical analysis.

The second example, provided in Listing 8-17, is oriented towards tables that contain LOB datatypes that need to be migrated and leverage the LOAD DATA INFILE utility. The types of files in most cases do not have any other lower level database logic other than storing LOB datatypes. The second example (see Listing 8-17) provides a comma delimited, double quotes encapsulated file that can then be loaded. There is a performance advantage with loading a file like this in comparison with performing the same data load using insert statements.

Both solutions use Dynamic SQL, providing for code reuse and simplification over having to write a different procedure for each table. The formatting is largely the difference between the two stored procedures. Both are written to accept the schema name, table name, and the directory to write to and are executed just like any other stored procedure. The code will need to be modified for any datatypes that are outside the scope of the sample stored procedures as provided. The files can then be transferred to the new DBMS server and loaded using the desired methods as mentioned.

Listing 8-16. Produces a Load File for Batch Loading as Insert Statements

```
CREATE OR REPLACE PROCEDURE GENERIC_EXPORT_V1
            (in_table in varchar2,
             in_owner varchar2,
             in_dir varchar2)
IS
v_file_name         varchar2(200);

sqlStr_hdr          varchar2(32767);
hdr_rslts           varchar2(32767);
hdr_cols            varchar2(32767);
sqlStr_data         varchar2(32767);

TYPE ref_cur is ref cursor;
out_file            UTL_FILE.FILE_TYPE;
v_timestamp_var     timestamp;
v_curid             NUMBER;
v_colid             NUMBER;
v_desctab           DBMS_SQL.DESC_TAB;
v_colname           varchar2(4096);
v_name_var          VARCHAR2(32767);

v_clob_var          CLOB;
v_cvchar   VARCHAR2(32767);
-- changed for lender_decision_doc
l_amt      number default 20000;
l_offset   number:= 1;
l_length   number;
```

```
v_pdf_var VARCHAR2(5);

v_blob_var BLOB;
blob_length     INTEGER;
v_buffer        RAW(32767);
chunk_size      BINARY_INTEGER := 18000;
v_bvchar        VARCHAR2(32000);
blob_position   INTEGER := 1;

v_num_var           NUMBER;
v_date_var          DATE;
v_row_num           NUMBER;
v_nothing           NUMBER;
v_count             number;
v_colcnt            number;
BEGIN
    v_file_name := (in_owner||'_'||lower(in_table)||'_migration.sql');
    out_file := UTL_FILE.fopen(in_dir,v_file_name,'w', 32767);

    execute immediate ('select count(*) from  all_tab_columns
    where owner = :1 and table_name = :2') into v_row_num using
    in_owner,in_table;
    sqlStr_hdr:='select column_name from all_tab_columns where
    owner = :1 and table_name = :2 order by column_id';
    v_colid := dbms_sql.open_cursor;
    dbms_sql.parse(v_colid,sqlStr_hdr,dbms_sql.native);
    DBMS_SQL.BIND_VARIABLE(v_colid, ':1', in_owner);
    DBMS_SQL.BIND_VARIABLE(v_colid, ':2', in_table);
    DBMS_SQL.DEFINE_COLUMN(v_colid,1,v_colname,1024);
    v_nothing := DBMS_SQL.EXECUTE(v_colid);
    v_count := 0;
    WHILE DBMS_SQL.FETCH_ROWS(v_colid) > 0 LOOP
        DBMS_SQL.COLUMN_VALUE(v_colid, 1, v_colname);
```

```
        hdr_cols := hdr_cols||v_colname;
        hdr_rslts := hdr_rslts||v_colname;
        v_count := v_count + 1;
        if (v_count < v_row_num) then
            hdr_cols := hdr_cols||',';
            hdr_rslts := hdr_rslts||',';
        end if;
    END LOOP;
    dbms_output.put_line(hdr_cols);
    dbms_output.put_line(hdr_rslts);

    DBMS_SQL.CLOSE_CURSOR(v_colid);
    sqlStr_data := 'select '||hdr_cols||' from '||in_
    owner||'.'||in_table;
    v_curid := dbms_sql.open_cursor;
    dbms_sql.parse(v_curid,sqlStr_data,dbms_sql.native);
    dbms_sql.describe_columns(v_curid,v_colcnt,v_desctab);

    FOR i IN 1 .. v_colcnt LOOP
        IF v_desctab(i).col_type = 2 THEN
            DBMS_SQL.DEFINE_COLUMN(v_curid, i, v_num_var);
        ELSIF v_desctab(i).col_type = 12 THEN
            DBMS_SQL.DEFINE_COLUMN(v_curid, i, v_date_var);
        ELSIF v_desctab(i).col_type = 180 THEN
            DBMS_SQL.DEFINE_COLUMN(v_curid, i, v_timestamp_var);
        ELSIF v_desctab(i).col_type = 112 THEN
            DBMS_SQL.DEFINE_COLUMN(v_curid,i,v_clob_var);
        ELSIF v_desctab(i).col_type = 113 THEN
            DBMS_SQL.DEFINE_COLUMN(v_curid,i,v_blob_var);
        ELSE
            DBMS_SQL.DEFINE_COLUMN(v_curid, i, v_name_var,1024);
        END IF;
    END LOOP;
```

```
v_row_num := dbms_sql.execute(v_curid);

v_count := 0;

WHILE DBMS_SQL.FETCH_ROWS(v_curid) > 0 LOOP
    utl_file.put(out_file,'insert into '||in_
    table||'('||hdr_rslts||') values (');
    FOR i IN 1 .. v_colcnt LOOP
        IF (v_desctab(i).col_type = 1) THEN
            DBMS_SQL.COLUMN_VALUE(v_curid, i, v_name_var);
            IF v_name_var IS NOT NULL THEN
                utl_file.put(out_file,""||replace(replace
                (v_name_var,"",""),'"','""')||"");
            ELSE
                utl_file.put(out_file,'NULL');
            END IF;
        ELSIF (v_desctab(i).col_type = 96) THEN
            DBMS_SQL.COLUMN VALUE(v_curid, i, v_name_var);
            IF v_num_var IS NOT NULL THEN
                utl_file.put(out_file,""||to_char(v_name_
                var)||"");
            ELSE
                utl_file.put(out_file,'NULL');
            END IF;
        ELSIF (v_desctab(i).col_type = 2) THEN
            DBMS_SQL.COLUMN_VALUE(v_curid, i, v_num_var);
            IF v_num_var IS NOT NULL THEN
                utl_file.put(out_file,""||to_char(v_num_
                var)||"");
            ELSE
                utl_file.put(out_file,'NULL');
            END IF;
```

```
ELSIF (v_desctab(i).col_type = 12) THEN
    DBMS_SQL.COLUMN_VALUE(v_curid, i, v_date_var);
    IF v_date_var IS NOT NULL THEN
      utl_file.put(out_file,""||to_char(v_date_
      var,'YYYY-MM-DD HH24:MI:SS')||"");
    ELSE
      utl_file.put(out_file,'NULL');
    END IF;
ELSIF (v_desctab(i).col_type = 180) THEN
    DBMS_SQL.COLUMN_VALUE(v_curid, i, v_timestamp_
    var);
    --dbms_output.put_line(v_date_var);
    IF v_timestamp_var IS NOT NULL THEN
      utl_file.put(out_file,""||to_char(v_
      timestamp_var,'YYYY-MM-DD HH24:MI:SS.FF')||"");
    ELSE
      utl_file.put(out_file,'NULL');
    END IF;
ELSIF (v_desctab(i).col_type = 112) THEN
    DBMS_SQL.COLUMN_VALUE(v_curid, i, v_clob_var);
    IF v_clob_var IS NOT NULL THEN
      utl_file.put(out_file,"");
      utl_file.fclose(out_file);
      out_file := utl_file.fopen(in_dir,v_file_name,
      'ab',32767);
      l_length := DBMS_LOB.getlength(v_clob_var);
      v_pdf_var := dbms_lob.substr(v_clob_var,4,1);
      while ( l_offset < l_length )
      loop
        v_cvchar := dbms_lob.substr(v_clob_var,l_amt,
        l_offset);
```

```
     if v_pdf_var = '%PDF' THEN
 utl_file.put_raw(out_file,utl_encode.base64_
 encode(utl_raw.cast_to_raw(v_cvchar)))
     else
       v_cvchar := replace(v_cvchar, '\',");
       v_cvchar := replace(v_cvchar,"", '\"');
       v_cvchar := replace(v_cvchar,'"', '\"');
       utl_file.put_raw(out_file,utl_raw.cast_to_
       raw(v_cvchar));
     end if;
     l_offset := l_offset + l_amt;
   end loop;
   v_pdf_var := NULL;
   l_offset := 1;
   utl_file.fclose(out_file);
   out_file := UTL_FILE.fopen(in_dir,v_file_name,
   'a', 32767);
   utl_file.put(out_file,"");
 ELSE
   utl_file.put(out_file,'NULL');
 END IF;
ELSIF (v_desctab(i).col_type = 113) THEN
   DBMS_SQL.COLUMN_VALUE(v_curid, i, v_blob_var);
   IF v_blob_var IS NOT NULL THEN
    utl_file.put(out_file,"");
    utl_file.fclose(out_file);
    out_file := utl_file.fopen(in_dir,v_file_name,
    'ab',32767);
    blob_length:=DBMS_LOB.GETLENGTH(v_blob_var);
    v_pdf_var := utl_raw.cast_to_varchar2(dbms_
    lob.substr(v_blob_var,4,1));
```

```
                WHILE blob_position <= blob_length LOOP
                IF blob_position + chunk_size - 1 > blob_
                length THEN
                chunk_size := blob_length - blob_position +
                1;
                END IF;
                DBMS_LOB.READ(v_blob_var, chunk_size, blob_
                position, v_buffer);
                v_bvchar := utl_raw.cast_to_varchar2(v_
                buffer);
                  v_bvchar := replace(v_bvchar,"", '\"');
                  v_bvchar := replace(v_bvchar,'"', '\"');
                  UTL_FILE.PUT_RAW(out_file, utl_raw.cast_
                  to_raw(v_bvchar));
                blob_position := blob_position + chunk_size;
                v_bvchar := NULL;
              END LOOP;
              chunk_size := 18000;
              blob_position := 1;
              v_pdf_var := NULL;
              utl_file.fclose(out_file);
              out_file := UTL_FILE.fopen(in_dir,v_file_name,
              'a', 32767);
              utl_file.put(out_file,"");
              ELSE
                utl_file.put(out_file,'NULL');
              END IF;
          END IF;
            v_count := v_count + 1;
        if (v_count < v_colcnt) then
            utl_file.put(out_file,',');
```

```
            elsif (v_count = v_colcnt) then
                utl_file.put_line(out_file,');');
            end if;
        END LOOP;
        v_count := 0;

        UTL_FILE.FFLUSH (out_file);

    END LOOP;
    DBMS_SQL.CLOSE_CURSOR(v_curid);
    utl_file.put_line(out_file,'commit;');
    UTL_FILE.FCLOSE (out_file);

END GENERIC_LOB_EXPORT_v1_9_1;
```

Listing 8-17. Produces a Load File for Batch Loading with LOAD DATA INFILE

```
CREATE OR REPLACE PROCEDURE GENERIC_LOB_INFILE
            (in_table in varchar2,
             in_owner varchar2,
             in_dir varchar2)
  IS

v_file_name           varchar2(200);
sqlStr_hdr            varchar2(32767);
hdr_rslts            varchar2(32767);
hdr_cols             varchar2(32767);
sqlStr_data          varchar2(32767);

TYPE ref_cur is ref cursor;
out_file             UTL_FILE.FILE_TYPE;
v_timestamp_var       timestamp;
v_curid               NUMBER;
```

127

```
v_colid                NUMBER;
v_desctab              DBMS_SQL.DESC_TAB;
v_colname              varchar2(4096);
v_name_var             VARCHAR2(32767);
v_clob_var             CLOB;
v_cvchar   VARCHAR2(32767);

l_amt      number default 20000;
l_offset   number:= 1;
l_length   number;
v_pdf_var VARCHAR2(5);

v_blob_var BLOB;
blob_length    INTEGER;
v_buffer       RAW(32767);
chunk_size     BINARY_INTEGER := 18000;
v_bvchar       VARCHAR2(32000);
blob_position  INTEGER := 1;
v_num_var              NUMBER;
v_date_var             DATE;
v_row_num              NUMBER;
v_nothing              NUMBER;
v_count                number;
v_colcnt               number;

BEGIN

v_file_name := (in_owner||'_'||lower(in_table)||'_migration.sql');
out_file := UTL_FILE.fopen(in_dir,v_file_name,'w', 32767);

execute immediate ('select count(*) from  all_tab_columns
where owner = :1 and table_name = :2') into v_row_num using
in_owner,in_table;
```

```
sqlStr_hdr:='select column_name from all_tab_columns where
owner = :1 and table_name = :2 order by column_id';
v_colid := dbms_sql.open_cursor;
dbms_sql.parse(v_colid,sqlStr_hdr,dbms_sql.native);

DBMS_SQL.BIND_VARIABLE(v_colid, ':1', in_owner);
DBMS_SQL.BIND_VARIABLE(v_colid, ':2', in_table);
DBMS_SQL.DEFINE_COLUMN(v_colid,1,v_colname,1024);

 v_nothing := DBMS_SQL.EXECUTE(v_colid);
 v_count := 0;

WHILE DBMS_SQL.FETCH_ROWS(v_colid) > 0 LOOP
        DBMS_SQL.COLUMN_VALUE(v_colid, 1, v_colname);
        hdr_cols := hdr_cols||v_colname;
        hdr_rslts := hdr_rslts||v_colname;
        v_count := v_count + 1;
        if (v_count < v_row_num) then
            hdr_cols := hdr_cols||',';
            hdr_rslts := hdr_rslts||',';
        end if;
    END LOOP;

    dbms_output.put_line(hdr_cols);
    dbms_output.put_line(hdr_rslts);
    DBMS_SQL.CLOSE_CURSOR(v_colid);
    sqlStr_data := 'select '||hdr_cols||' from '||in_
    owner||'.'||in_table;
    v_curid := dbms_sql.open_cursor;
    dbms_sql.parse(v_curid,sqlStr_data,dbms_sql.native);
    dbms_sql.describe_columns(v_curid,v_colcnt,v_desctab);
```

```
    FOR i IN 1 .. v_colcnt LOOP
        IF v_desctab(i).col_type = 2 THEN
            DBMS_SQL.DEFINE_COLUMN(v_curid, i, v_num_var);
        ELSIF v_desctab(i).col_type = 12 THEN
            DBMS_SQL.DEFINE_COLUMN(v_curid, i, v_date_var);
        ELSIF v_desctab(i).col_type = 180 THEN
            DBMS_SQL.DEFINE_COLUMN(v_curid, i, v_timestamp_var);
        ELSIF v_desctab(i).col_type = 112 THEN
            DBMS_SQL.DEFINE_COLUMN(v_curid,i,v_clob_var);
        ELSIF v_desctab(i).col_type = 113 THEN
            DBMS_SQL.DEFINE_COLUMN(v_curid,i,v_blob_var);
        ELSE
            DBMS_SQL.DEFINE_COLUMN(v_curid, i, v_name_var,1024);
        END IF;
    END LOOP;

    v_row_num := dbms_sql.execute(v_curid);
    v_count := 0;
    WHILE DBMS_SQL.FETCH_ROWS(v_curid) > 0 LOOP
        FOR i IN 1 .. v_colcnt LOOP
            IF (v_desctab(i).col_type = 1) THEN
                DBMS_SQL.COLUMN_VALUE(v_curid, i, v_name_var);
                IF v_name_var IS NOT NULL THEN
                  utl_file.put(out_file,'"'||replace(replace
                  (v_name_var,"",""""),'"','""')||'"');
                ELSE
                  utl_file.put(out_file,'NULL');
                END IF;
            ELSIF (v_desctab(i).col_type = 96) THEN
                DBMS_SQL.COLUMN_VALUE(v_curid, i, v_name_var);
                IF v_num_var IS NOT NULL THEN
```

```
      utl_file.put(out_file,'"'||to_char(v_name_
      var)||'"');
    ELSE
      utl_file.put(out_file,'NULL');
    END IF;
ELSIF (v_desctab(i).col_type = 2) THEN
    DBMS_SQL.COLUMN_VALUE(v_curid, i, v_num_var);
    IF v_num_var IS NOT NULL THEN
      utl_file.put(out_file,'"'||to_char(v_num_
      var)||'"');
    ELSE
      utl_file.put(out_file,'NULL');
    END IF;
ELSIF (v_desctab(i).col_type = 12) THEN
    DBMS_SQL.COLUMN_VALUE(v_curid, i, v_date_var);
    IF v_date_var IS NOT NULL THEN
      utl_file.put(out_file,'"'||to_char(v_date_var,
      'YYYY-MM-DD HH24:MI:SS')||'"');
    ELSE
      utl_file.put(out_file,'NULL');
    END IF;
ELSIF (v_desctab(i).col_type = 180) THEN
    DBMS_SQL.COLUMN_VALUE(v_curid, i, v_timestamp_
    var);
    IF v_timestamp_var IS NOT NULL THEN
      utl_file.put(out_file,'"'||to_char(v_timestamp_
      var,'YYYY-MM-DD HH24:MI:SS.FF')||'"');
    ELSE
      utl_file.put(out_file,'NULL');
    END IF;
```

```
ELSIF (v_desctab(i).col_type = 112) THEN
    DBMS_SQL.COLUMN_VALUE(v_curid, i, v_clob_var);
    IF v_clob_var IS NOT NULL THEN
      utl_file.put(out_file,'"');
      utl_file.fclose(out_file);
      out_file := utl_file.fopen(in_dir,v_file_name,
      'ab',32767);
      l_length := DBMS_LOB.getlength(v_clob_var);
      v_pdf_var := dbms_lob.substr(v_clob_var,4,1);
      while ( l_offset < l_length )
      loop
       v_cvchar := dbms_lob.substr(v_clob_var,
       l_amt,l_offset);
        v_cvchar := replace(v_cvchar, '\',");
        v_cvchar := replace(v_cvchar,"", '\"');
        v_cvchar := replace(v_cvchar,'"', '\"');
        utl_file.put_raw(out_file,utl_raw.cast_to_
        raw(v_cvchar));
       l_offset := l_offset + l_amt;
      end loop;
      v_pdf_var := NULL
      l_offset := 1;
      utl_file.fclose(out_file);
      out_file := UTL_FILE.fopen(in_dir,v_file_name,
      'a', 32767);
      utl_file.put(out_file,'"');
    ELSE
      utl_file.put(out_file,'NULL');
    END IF;
```

```
ELSIF (v_desctab(i).col_type = 113) THEN
    DBMS_SQL.COLUMN_VALUE(v_curid, i, v_blob_var);
    IF v_blob_var IS NOT NULL THEN
     utl_file.put(out_file,'"');
     utl_file.fclose(out_file);
     out_file := utl_file.fopen(in_dir,v_file_name,
     'ab',32767);
     blob_length:=DBMS_LOB.GETLENGTH(v_blob_var);
     v_pdf_var := utl_raw.cast_to_varchar2(dbms_
     lob.substr(v_blob_var,4,1));
     WHILE blob_position <= blob_length LOOP
        IF blob_position + chunk_size - 1 > blob_
        length THEN
        chunk_size := blob_length - blob_position + 1;
        END IF;
        DBMS_LOB.READ(v_blob_var, chunk_size,
        blob_position, v_buffer);
        v_bvchar := utl_raw.cast_to_varchar2
        (v_buffer);
         v_bvchar := replace(v_bvchar,"", '\"');
         v_bvchar := replace(v_bvchar,'"', '\"');
         v_bvchar := replace(v_bvchar,',', '\,');
        UTL_FILE.PUT_RAW(out_file, utl_raw.cast_
        to_raw(v_bvchar));

        blob_position := blob_position + chunk_size;
        v_bvchar := NULL;
    END LOOP;
    chunk_size := 18000;
    blob_position := 1;
    v_pdf_var := NULL;
    utl_file.fclose(out_file);
```

```
              out_file := UTL_FILE.fopen(in_dir,v_file_name,
              'a', 32767);
              utl_file.put(out_file,'"');
              ELSE
                utl_file.put(out_file,'NULL');
              END IF;
          END IF;
              v_count := v_count + 1;
          if (v_count < v_colcnt) then
              utl_file.put(out_file,',');
          elsif (v_count = v_colcnt) then
              utl_file.put_line(out_file,");
              utl_file.put_line(out_file,'RECEND');
          end if;
      END LOOP;
      v_count := 0;
      UTL_FILE.FFLUSH (out_file);
   END LOOP;
   DBMS_SQL.CLOSE_CURSOR(v_curid);
   UTL_FILE.FCLOSE (out_file);

END GENERIC_LOB_INFILE_v1;
```

APPENDIX A

Open Source Continuum

The Open Source community has gone full circle over the past few decades, from first being considered as hobbyist software that was buggy and not to be considered as professionally ready for prime time to making inroads into a myriad of businesses, governments, and organizations. With solution offerings that many times surpass the quality and capabilities of the most costly and proprietary based systems, Open Source solutions have proved themselves capable. From professional grade operating systems that are taking over in the world's data centers to business office oriented tools like spreadsheets and document editors, the Open Source world of solutions has matured and become a mainstay; not bad for once-labeled products of amateur hobby.

Large proprietary software and solution providers that had once dismissed Open Source solutions as inferior amateur products have been forced to come to terms. In the raw actuality the term Open Source is a more modern term for software sharing and collaborative development principles that have been around since the advent of the term software. It has become common knowledge that in the early days of computing, virtually all software was created by academics and researchers in the corporate world who were all working collaboratively and sharing the results of their endeavors openly and freely. It is literally amazing that the digital and computing world that modern times have experienced came from such humble beginnings.

© William Wood 2019
W. Wood, *Migrating to MariaDB*, https://doi.org/10.1007/978-1-4842-3997-1

Open Source in the Data Center

If there was a defining moment in time that truly indicated the beginnings of the modern advent of what we now call Open Source, one could target the year 1991 as just such a moment. This was when Linus Torvalds released the first version of his Open Source Operating System, effectively going on to be named Linux, which was based in part on System V Unix and written in the C programming language. There are many other software solutions and operating systems of note that came before Linux; however, when looking back over time and comparing to what is driving the current data center and having a monumental impact on modern computing today, the Linux OS stands out.

Originally released just as an OS kernel, it has aged gracefully and migrated into the OS of choice in computing industry data centers around the world. Initially it took the majority of web-based server roles in large part to other Open Source driven works like Perl, PHP, and MySQL. Now the Linux OS has become the go-to for web hosting and web development for which terms like LAMP Stack were coined, which referred to the combination of Linux Apache MySQL and PHP/Perl. The population of Linux servers has literally exploded over the years, supplanting such mainstays as HP-UX, Windows Server, and Solaris just to name a few, to the point that in some statistics it's holding 60% to 70% of the rack space in web hosting environments. With the web hosting market as just the beginning, the Linux OS with its many distributions (distros) has not stopped there and has moved into enterprise application hosting as well.

There are several Linux distros to choose from; however, we are going to maintain our focus on the one pulled from the story about Vernon and his team at Financial Widgets Plus (FWP), RedHat. The RedHat organization is one of the largest success stories coming from the Open Source arena, both commercial and community based, via their Enterprise Linux and Fedora versions, respectively. Their team chose RedHat Enterprise Linux (RHEL) as their OS of choice when replacing their HP-UX environments, experiencing improvements in both performance and ease of maintenance when it came to hosting their Oracle RAC environment. Oracle even has released their own distribution, effectively named Oracle Linux, which has a striking resemblance to RedHat's RHEL with a kernel that is reportedly enhanced specifically for running the Oracle DBMS and similar products. This has resulted in wild speculation in media circles and authorships of a bit of hard feelings between the two organizations, but this will be left to the individual reader to interpret in regard to any significance therein.

RHEL is a rock solid and very well supported commercial version of the RedHat distribution, and along with many other distribution providers they have in recent years begun to supplant the historical inclusion of the MySQL ODBMS with their newer releases with MariaDB. This aversion to Oracle products can be interpreted in many ways as a storyline similar to that of the fictional account of the FWP team in regard to the fictional business practices alluded to by the Oracle Corporation in recent years. This is left to the readership to make their own decisions, do their own research, and form their own opinions on such matters. As to why businesses make the choices they do, in many cases, just as in Financial Widget Plus's case, the primary driver is that it made good business sense to migrate away from their high-cost proprietary legacy database solution.

Anyone would be hard pressed to claim that Oracle has not developed a less than desirable reputation over the years, which comes with growth and sometimes can be a by-product of success as well as competition driven. The fact is Oracle and their perceived business practices had a positive effect on the Open Source community with their purchase of Sun Microsystems, and by inclusion MySQL, in 2010. This was the catalyst for the creation of the MySQL fork by Michael Widenius that has become a perfectly viable replacement for Oracle's own Enterprise Edition DBMS, with the inclusion and support of encryption for data at rest released in version 10.1.

With many improvements since release 10.1, MariaDB has grown their solution into a fully dependable, professionally driven and secure database solution that is an entirely Open Source commercial product. There is a magnanimous amount of excitement growing in the computing industry about MariaDB, and it's future appears to be limitless with the strides in market share and improvements the folks there are making on a daily bases. Where RedHat has taken over the data centers in recent years, MariaDB now stands poised to take over the data.

Entrepreneurial Limits of Big Name Proprietary Systems

The costs as calculated and used by Vernon in the fictional example for FWP used pricing metrics that were derived from publicly available pricing lists published by the Oracle Corporation. These numbers beg the question as to how would any small business, enterprising startup, or in the case of an existing small company like FWP who is trying to expand, afford to do so. These costs are amazing in comparison and could easily break a business just from the initial upfront costs. This is where the commercially available versions of software from the Open Source community are not only viable solutions, but solutions that will assuredly garner a substantially growing market share in the future.

The entrepreneurial spirit and competition are easily squashed by high-priced and closed proprietary solutions that can run into the millions of dollars in cost just for the first five years of a new business. This is money that would be well spent in generating more revenue to help a business succeed in the first few years of their incarnation, and this is something that closed system proprietors like the Oracle Corporation do not seem to understand the concepts of and where companies like RedHat and MariaDB stand to make their mark. They see the bottom line relying on the sole benefit of the short-term hustle by charging as much as possible without benefit of looking at the longer term arrangement. What is suggested here is counterintuitive to the age old management and business practices that have been employed historically; however, the logic is sound.

Revenue generation and earnings impact can be expanded greatly over time with an approach centered on creating and developing a business relationship using a much more affordable pricing model to grow your earnings over time. This can be easily modeled using the fictional FWP and the information garnered from their experience. According to the Small Business Administration (SBA) one out of five businesses fail in the first year and approximately 50% fail within the first five years, so comparing Oracle's pricing model with that of MariaDB we have the following calculated costs for five years:

- Oracle: $1,562,280

- MariaDB: $187,500

- Difference: $1,374,780

This is a huge discrepancy of $1,374,780 comparing a standalone three-node setup in a clustered database environment. Imagine what any business could do with that extra money, much less an enterprising business bent on success. That would be money that could be reinvested back into the business for marketing, resources, staffing, and various other methods used to obtain more customers and augment existing solutions. This amount of savings being put back into the business in a beneficial manner could very well mean the difference between success and failure. In the end, would it be enough to improve the SBA statistics is not easily answered; however, it is certainly food for thought and a topic to be explored.

There is always a flip side to any kind of extruded benefit from this logic and that is that if 50% of all business are going to fail, then it would be better to reap the highest potential earnings possible for a large entity such as the Oracle Corporation. In this scenario, only one entity benefits from this strategy and can add another island to their holdings, whereas with the logic being presented the benefits are spread out exponentially along with the potential for a higher business success rate not only with the business, but also with their vendors, including their ODBMS vendor. With more revenue to invest in driving solutions to market resulting in more customers, and possibly providing more services to existing customers through increased product offerings, this will create a ratio to include having to increase and maximize their database footprint to account for this growth.

This is where the Open Source Continuum exists in all of its disjoint glory from the closed source proprietary systems. It allows for maximizing success due to lowered costs, while maximizing its own future at the same time in doing so, if leveraged appropriately with good business practices. Exploring this is as easy as envisioning a new start-up company, calling it OSC in honor of the Open Source Continuum, and analyzing the potential in a monetary timeline starting at the end of its first year.

Exploring the state of OSC, they effactually have broken even after inking a five-year deal with MariaDB for their database service on the single three-node production cluster leaving them over a million dollars to reinvest back into the business the second year. OSC has also contracted to provide their service to 55 customers in their first year, and they have found that they can easily run an optimum tuned database count of 50 customers on their three-node cluster with no performance impact. The state of the business is as such:

- Funds being reinvested the second year: $1,374,780

- Current number of customers: 60

- Customers in various stages of contract negotiations or deployment: 12

- Additional potential customers: 6

Let's imagine that OSC decides to spend part of their operating funds on marketing, attending conferences, and exploring additional business relationships in order to expand their business and need to add additional clusters to meet these needs. With a large influx in business comes the need to add additional database resources, thus expanding the footprint and increasing licensing requirements for MariaDB. This is a successful business model where many more benefit.

At the end of year two, OSC has expanded their customer base significantly and is becoming quite the success story. Their current state of business is:

- Current number of customers: 110

- Customers in various stages of on boarding: 24

- Potential customers: 16

OSC has had to expand their MariaDB licensing to account for this and now has three production clusters running. This has tripled their new ODBMS footprint and they are now spending almost $600,000 with their new vendor for licensing and support. In the meantime, the MariaDB organization has experienced corresponding growth as well, which means hiring more staff to handle the increase and an increase in revenue.

It is easy to see that Open Source embraces the entrepreneurial spirit and provides solutions that would otherwise be beyond reach. From the developer working in her/his free time on an idea to add to the code base, to the small start-up, and reaching all the way to the largest organizations the solutions that were once thought of as amateur are coming into their own. From RedHat taking over the data centers to MariaDB taking on the niche that a company like Oracle has held onto for so many years, it is an exciting time to be working in the technology sector.

Where Is Open Source Not Viable

All of this begs the question, is there anywhere that Open Source technologies cannot be considered a viable solution, and that answer is becoming harder to get to every day. The advent of taking Open Source solutions into the business world via commercially branded and supported versions, that by the way are still open, has changed the viewpoint to where proprietary closed systems are not seen as the only answer anymore. Community driven projects can be leveraged for virtually anything and their potential is limitless.

There will almost always be proprietary systems and code, as that is also part of the entrepreneurial spirit as well. In many cases intellectual rights to ingenious ideas, designs, and concepts do need to be protected and closely guarded, as they may very well relate to a business or entity's survival and earnings potential. The optimum solution is one that employs Open Source to drive these types of ideas and designs. Stealing an often heard buzzword, we could call these hybrid Open Source solutions.

An arguable point might be that highly secure systems for military and government use might not be a good area for Open Source solutions; however, that actually flies in the face of the entire concept behind it. It has been the author's opinion for many years that if someone can build something, they can certainly break it down, and since many of the Open Source solutions come from the global community there is certainly concern with terrorism, security breaches, and data theft. This is true with virtually any software that is pirated, and by using reverse engineering methodologies, even with closed proprietary systems. However, with Open Source solutions the code is much more available with potentially less time involved in finding a security flaw. On the other side of that same coin is that these solutions are Open Source and can be modified, ported, and expanded from their original base to add in additional security, validations, and capabilities.

In the early days of what we now refer to as Open Source, the risks were potentially very high with many solutions being buggy, lacking thorough documentation, and in essence much broader to an organization. Commercially marketed and supported solutions have mitigated many of these issues with dedicated resources from the vendors in regard to developers and engineers augmented by services and offerings such as 24/7 technical support, training, certifications, and even remote administration available to augment one's internal staff.

Benefits of Open Source

The benefits of Open Source as presented are boundless. Even though it has been around a very long time and was the basis of almost all initial software development, it has made a resurgence and has come full circle into its own with what are becoming standard deployments and go-to solutions. The growth in open source offerings will continue, with their commercially offered counterparts being the springboard into mainstream adoption.

The entrepreneurial spirit of open source solutions opens up the same spirits in small companies and start-ups that can leverage these capable but lower cost solutions to get into the marketplace with their products and thrive. This has been proven time and time again over the past two decades as open solutions have taken over, as vast amounts of the daily processing that occurs over the World Wide Web is being performed by solutions like Apache, MySQL, PostGres, Perl, PHP, and Linux. Fortunes have been made with online stores that initially had low cost and short implementation times to get up and running due to leveraging open source solutions to drive these virtual store fronts.

Anyone with a desire to learn technology can do so with open source technologies; whether they want to be a programmer, database administrator, web developer, systems administrator, or anything in between, the opportunity is there. It is free, it is open, and all one has to do is download it. The avenues are there to learn the software and even become a contributor for anyone who has an interest. The same cannot be said for proprietary closed systems; not that they don't have their place, but it isn't as easy to get into the nuts and bolts and improve them.

Index

A, B

Advanced Security Option (ASO),
    5, 13, 14, 21, 24
Agile methodologies, 81
Application code
    daemons, 44
    encrypted data, 43
    MariaDB, 45
    Maxscale, 44
    on-site training, 45
    OSDBMS, 43
    proxy server, 44
    SQL, 43
    structured data, 43
Architect team, 98
Audits
    compliance
        encryption at rest, 36
        encryption at
          transmission, SSL, 36
        PAM, 36
        plugin, 36
        RSA, 36
    database, 24
    database footprint, 26
    data security, 19
    encryption methods

        algorithms, 26
        asymmetric keys, 22
        cryptoperiod, 22
        data at rest, 23
        data in transmission, 23
        keys, 22
          rotating keys, 23–24
    MySQL, 24, 30
    PCI DSS, 21
    security breach, 19
    server license scope, 26
    SSAE 16, 19, 21
    standardized solutions, 25
Automation, 74, 85
    Agile, 86
    bottlenecks, 87
    computers, 85
    CSV, 86
    customized, 86
    database team, 87
    development team, 85
    DevOps, 86
    encapsulated fields, 86
    human error, 85
    IETF, 86
    methodology, 86
    principles, 85
    process steps, 85

W, X

Y, Z

Printed in the United States
By Bookmasters

Printed in the United States
By Bookmasters